What is 3

This, our second title in the well-received "3D ORIGAMI" series, invites you to learn an innovative approach to the craft of making authentic origami. Each of the intricate projects begins with a small rectangular piece of paper folded into a tiny, "magical" triangle. By combining lots of such "magical" triangles in various positions, you can build up ornamental objects that are solid and three dimensional. It's so much fun you won't believe what you have created before you know it.

IT ALL STARS WITH THE BASIC TRIANGLE

Make around 70 triangles, and construct a small project such as a Piggyback Turtle. By the time it is completed, you will understand how to make use of the unique structure of the triangle; the three different sides and three different points. By altering the direction in which the triangles are joined, you'll be able to make any shape you can imagine. In other words, with 3D origami, practice makes perfect. See page 25 for more details.

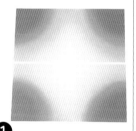

❶ Use one half of a square origami paper.

❷ Fold in half to make a thinner rectangle.

❸ Fold in half, this time in the other direction.

❹ Fold up upper flap so its bottom edge aligns with the left side.

❺ Turn over and fold the other flap in the same manner.

❻ Open as shown.

❼ Fold down upper corners diagonally.

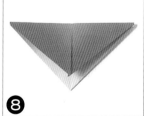

❽ Fold down in half.

❾ Fold in half again for a completed basic triangle.

●**Instructions shown here are designed for commercial origami paper. For different shaped paper, see pages 26-27.**

RECYCLING FUN

Basket
See page 23.

Warrior's Helmet
See page 15.

Decorative Bowl
See page 23.

Star-shaped Basket
See page 23.

◆scrap paper

❶

Fold in half.

❷

Fold in half again.

❸

Unfold and bring up bottom edges to align at the center. Turn over.

❹

Fold down upper corners diagonally.

Why not give life to papers that are destined to be thrown away? Glossy catalogs, wrapping paper, flyers, or even magazine paper will make unexpectedly shaded, one-of-a-kind ornaments. These papers are heavy weight and perfect for objects. Plan your own color scheme by choosing coordinating page, or be adventurous for a surprising result.

Pot Cover
See page 22.

Flopping Crane
See page 12.

Flatback Turtle
See page 10.

Vase
See page 22.

❺ Fold down in half.

❻ Fold in half again for a completed triangular piece.

❼ Make a number of these pieces.

❽ Interlock them one by one to construct a figure.

3

◆ BASIC HORIZONTAL ASSEMBLY

Here is an easily assembled work that extends in one direction. Just remember to set the pocket edge of the piece to face the same side as you join them. A charming turtle will be created in no time with 70 prepared triangles.

#2 Piggyback Turtles, black
See page 31 for detailed instructions.

#1 Piggyback Turtles, pink
See page 31 for detailed instructions.

The turtle has been a symbol of longevity in Japan as seen by the adage: The crane lives a thousand years, the turtle, ten thousand years.

❶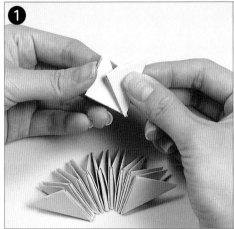

Take 9 pieces. Apply glue onto the pointed tip of each piece, and stick together.

❷

The first row is completed. Be sure to glue the points that connect the pockets.

❸

Interlock second row pieces by inserting the peak of each first row into each pocket.

❹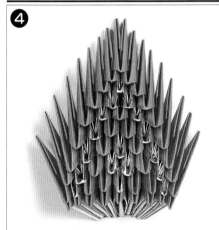

Interlock 11 rows in all, referring to the color chart on page 31.

❺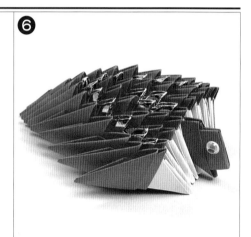

Make head using 2 pieces.

❻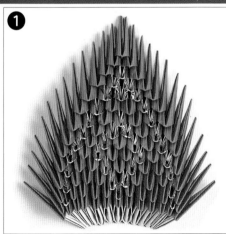

Attach the head to the body for completed turtle.

❶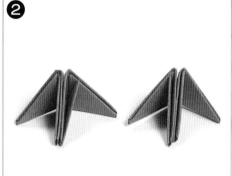

Make body in the same manner as BABY TURTLE.

❷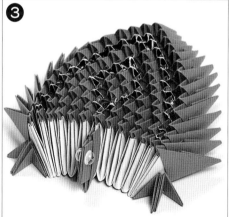

Make feet by gluing 2 pieces each.

❸

Attach the feet and head for completed turtle.

◆ CIRCULAR ASSEMBLY

When you join the pieces in a circle, they make a base for most three-dimensional objects that extend upward. Once you have learned the trick of the triangular piece, e.g. how each side of the triangle works, you can construct any shape you fancy. Start with small projects such as these doll-shaped containers.

#3 Japanese Dolls
See page 35 for detailed instructions.

March 3 is Japan's Doll Festival, to wish that all girls grow up healthy. This pair of dolls represents an ancient emperor and empress, and is a must decoration for any home with daughters. This cute version can be used as a container for candies.

❶

Join 2 pieces by stacking a new piece onto adjacent points. Hold the new piece pocket side down and the right-angle point away from you. Make 12 of this.

❷ This sample shows different colors for comprehension. In the actual project, use a single shade.

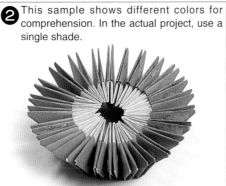

Join two units by stacking on another piece. Then add another unit and join in the same manner until 25 pieces are used for each 1st and 2nd row. Reinforce the base by turning over and interlocking a further 25 pieces.

❸

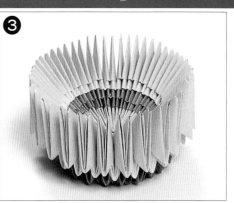

In the same manner, join 25 pieces on rows 3 to 5.

❹

For row 6, change color according to the chart on page 35. This is a frontal view.

❺

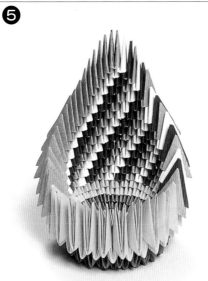

Work rows 6 to 20 referring to the color chart.

❻

Attach head for completed doll.

EMPEROR

Make an *eboshi* hat for the emperor.

EMPRESS

Attach hair and place a golden crane on it.

GOOD LUCK ORNAMENTS

#4 A Dragon Couple
See page 28 for instructions

#5 Flying Dragon
See page 28 for instructions

#6 God-of-Thunder Dragon

See page 28 for instructions
A scrap paper of a forest picture is used for the
body. (Instructions are not included.)

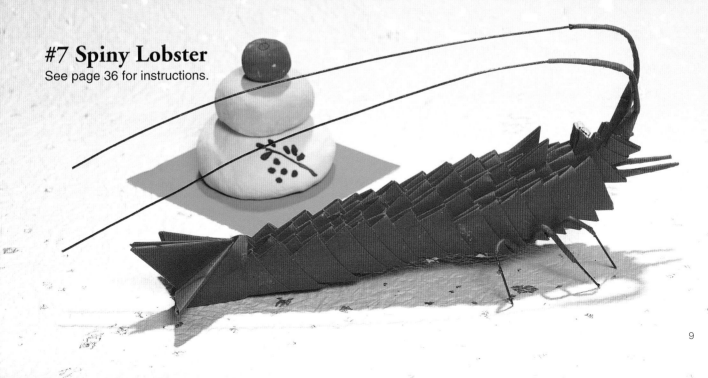

#7 Spiny Lobster

See page 36 for instructions.

Long Life Turtle
See page 32 for instructions.

#9

#8

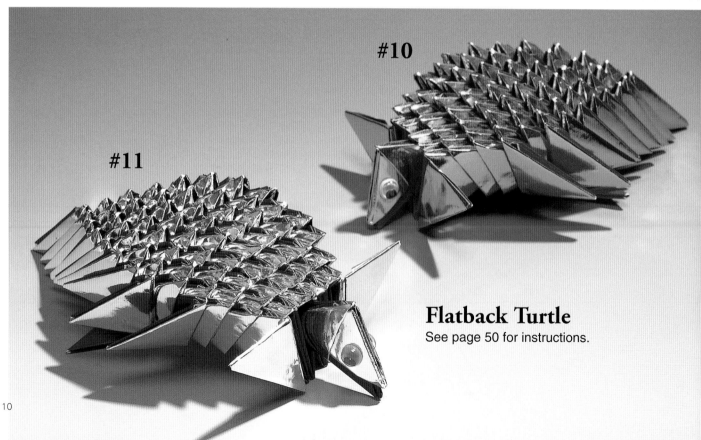

#10

#11

Flatback Turtle
See page 50 for instructions.

#12 Treasure Boat
See page 40 for instructions.

Treasure Boat with Seven Deities of Good Luck
See page 38 for instructions.

#13

#14

11

#15 Flopping Crane
See page 44 for instructions.

#16 Sitting Crane
See page 42 for instructions.

#18 Japanese Crane
See page 46 for instructions.

#17 Young Crane
See page 46 for instructions.

#20 Swan
See page 47 for instructions.

#19 Chicken
See page 48 for instructions.

13

#21 Elderly Owl Couple
See pages 57-59 for instructions.

Traditional Japanese Hand Ball
See page 49 for instructions.

#22

#23

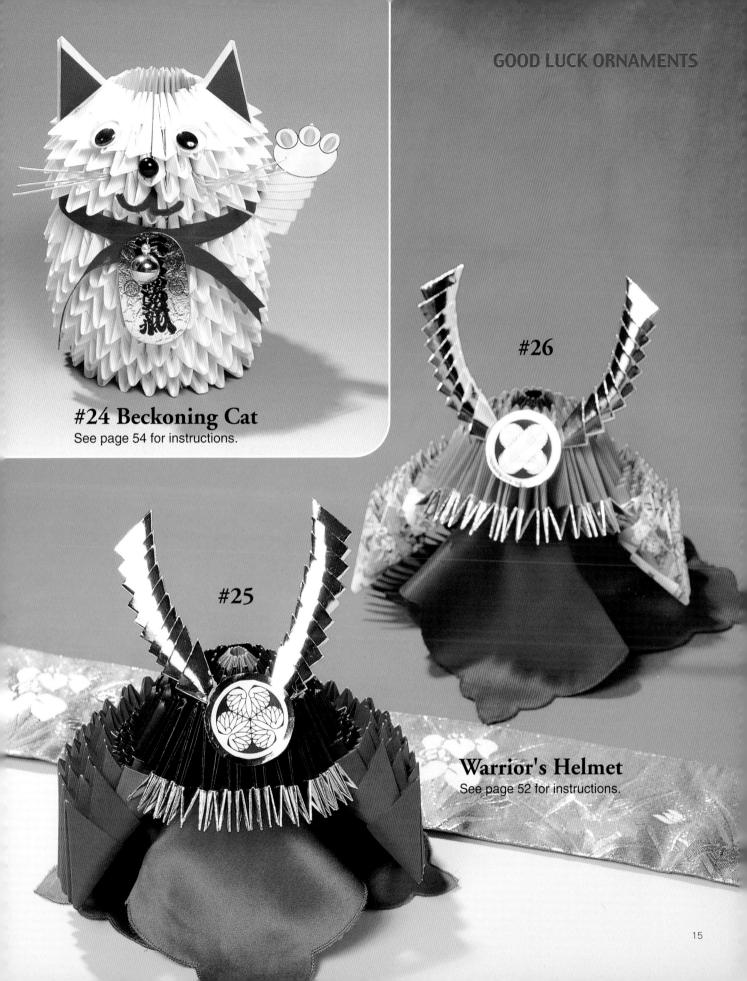

#24 Beckoning Cat
See page 54 for instructions.

#26

#25

Warrior's Helmet
See page 52 for instructions.

15

ADORABLE ANIMALS

#28 Panda Bear
See page 64 for instructions.

#27 Puppy
See page 62 for instructions.

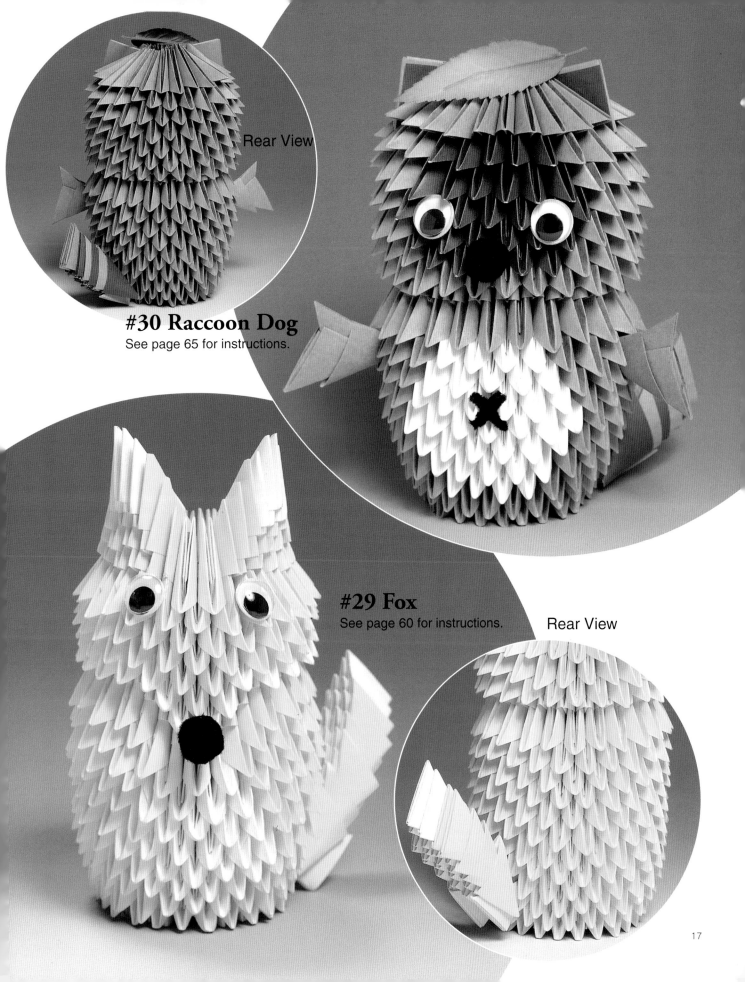

Rear View

#30 Raccoon Dog
See page 65 for instructions.

#29 Fox
See page 60 for instructions.

Rear View

#31 Black Owls
See page 68 for instructions.

Owl Family

#32 Blue Owls
See page 70 for instructions.

Baby Owl
See page 66 for instructions.

#34

#33

Alley Cat
See page 56 for instructions.

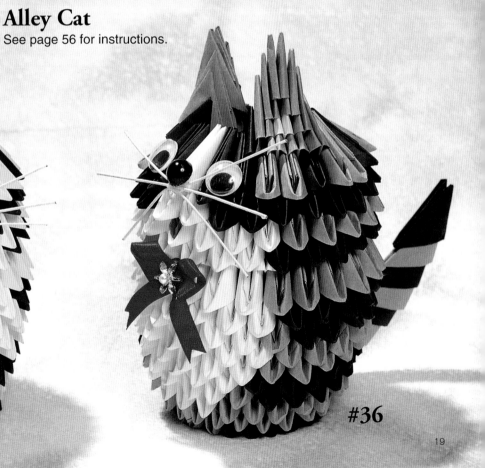

#35

#36

#37

#38

Rainbow Swan
See page 76 for instructions.

Black Swan
See page 74 for instructions.

#39

#40

#41 Peacock

See pages 71-73 for instructions.

Side View

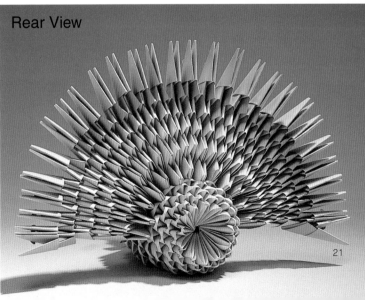

Rear View

21

DECORATIVE CONTAINERS

One of the unique advantages of this origami is that you can adjust the size accordingly. Just loosen or tighten the piecing so that the inner edges fit to a jar, bottle, or whatever you have at hand. Glue the pieces together, and voila! A stiff and stable container stands there alone in an artistic form.

#43 Vase
See page 81 for instructions.

#42 Pot Cover
See page 80 for instructions.

#44 Vase
See page 81 for instructions.

#45 Vase
See page 78 for instructions.

#50 Star-Shaped Basket

See page 82 for instructions.

#46 Basket

See page 79 for instructions.

#48
Decorative Bowl

See page 82 for instructions.

#47 Basket

See page 79 for instructions.

#49 Star-Shaped Basket

See page 82 for instructions.

#52 Basket with Handle
See page 86 for instructions.

#51 Vase with Rim
See page 87 for instructions.

#53 Flower-Shaped Basket
See page 84 for instructions

HOW TO PREPARE TRIANGULAR PIECES:

We have come up with three different ways to fold triangles, from which you can choose depending on the paper to be folded. In other words, you don't need to be very picky about the size of paper. Practice each method to gain confidence in transforming the paper into your favorite figures.

TYPE "A" TRIANGLE

This is mainly for the users of square origami paper, which, when halved, has an exact 1:2 ratio of short side to long side.

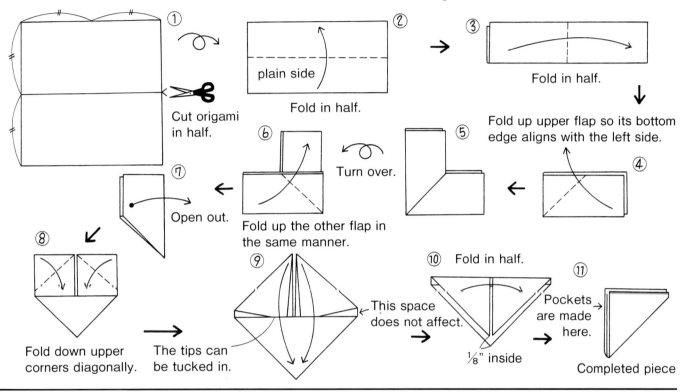

① Cut origami in half.

② Fold in half. plain side

③ Fold in half.

④ Fold up upper flap so its bottom edge aligns with the left side.

⑤

⑥ Turn over. Fold up the other flap in the same manner.

⑦ Open out.

⑧ Fold down upper corners diagonally.

The tips can be tucked in.

⑨ This space does not affect.

⑩ Fold in half. ⅛" inside

⑪ Pockets are made here.

Completed piece

◆BASIC ASSEMBLY◆

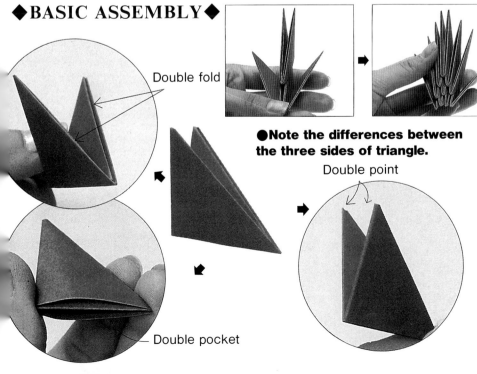

Double fold

Double pocket

●Note the differences between the three sides of triangle.

Double point

In most cases, you join pieces by inserting the double points of two pieces into the double pocket of another piece: First, hold two pieces together, double points up, and then stack on a new piece by inserting the center two points into the double pocket of the new piece. This way the adjacent points of the first two pieces are fastened by the new piece, which at the same time makes a second row. The direction of the piecing depends on each project.

TYPE "B" TRIANGLE

A triangle created with a slightly "longer" rectangle than type A. This 1:2+ ratio rectangle is suitable when using B4 size or scrap paper.
You can mix and match any type of triangles in a single project as long as the short side measures the same.

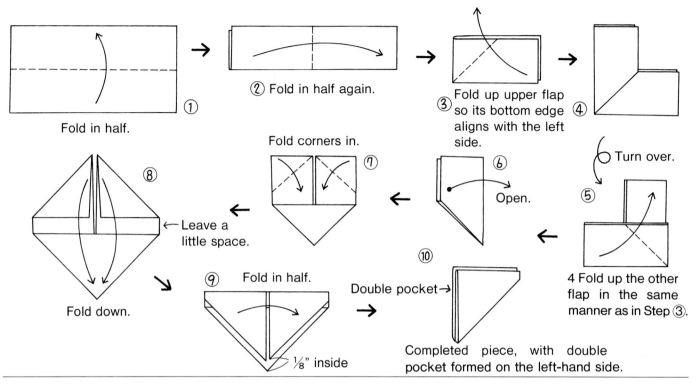

① Fold in half.

② Fold in half again.

③ Fold up upper flap so its bottom edge aligns with the left side.

④

⑤ Turn over.

4 Fold up the other flap in the same manner as in Step ③.

⑥ Open.

⑦ Fold corners in.

⑧ ← Leave a little space.

Fold down.

⑨ Fold in half. ⅛" inside

⑩ Double pocket →

Completed piece, with double pocket formed on the left-hand side.

TYPE "C" TRIANGLE

This triangle is created with somewhat "shorter" rectangle that has 1:2⁻ ratio of short side to long side. In this method, as the paper is layered only partially and the peak seems "trimmed," you will find this type easier to assemble. Recommended to users of thick paper, or when a sturdy look is required.

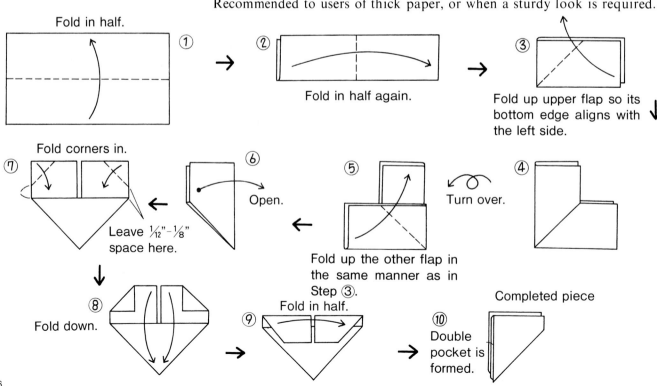

① Fold in half.

② Fold in half again.

③ Fold up upper flap so its bottom edge aligns with the left side.

④

⑤ Turn over. Fold up the other flap in the same manner as in Step ③.

⑥ Open.

⑦ Fold corners in. Leave 1/12"–⅛" space here.

⑧ Fold down.

⑨ Fold in half.

⑩ Double pocket is formed. Completed piece

PRACTICAL EXAMPLE FOR CUTTING B4 SIZE PAPER INTO TYPE B RECTANGLES

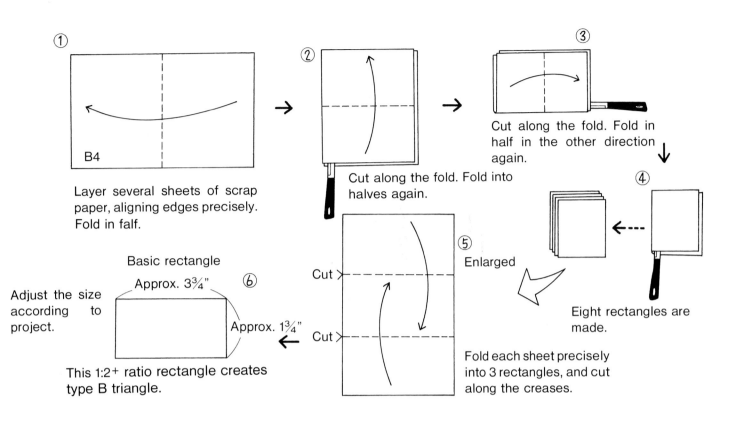

① Layer several sheets of scrap paper, aligning edges precisely. Fold in falf.

② Cut along the fold. Fold into halves again.

③ Cut along the fold. Fold in half in the other direction again.

④

Eight rectangles are made.

⑤ Enlarged

Fold each sheet precisely into 3 rectangles, and cut along the creases.

Cut

Cut

⑥ Basic rectangle

Approx. 3¾"

Approx. 1¾"

Adjust the size according to project.

This 1:2⁺ ratio rectangle creates type B triangle.

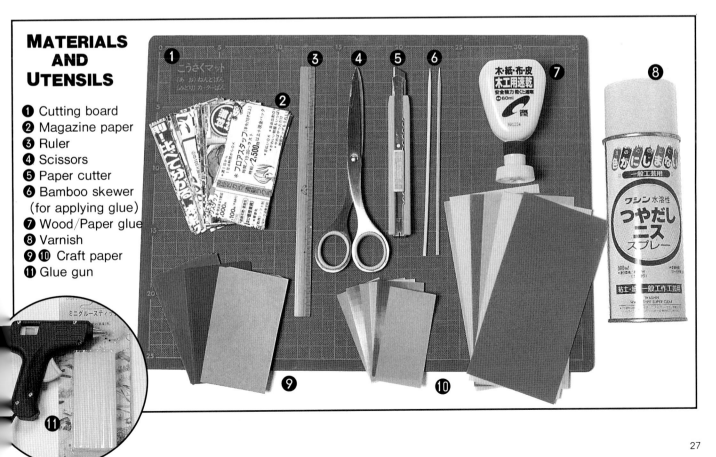

MATERIALS AND UTENSILS

❶ Cutting board
❷ Magazine paper
❸ Ruler
❹ Scissors
❺ Paper cutter
❻ Bamboo skewer
  (for applying glue)
❼ Wood/Paper glue
❽ Varnish
❾❿ Craft paper
⓫ Glue gun

Finished size: $4\frac{1}{2}'' \times 14''$

Paper materials per dragon (craft paper)

96 $2'' \times 3\frac{1}{2}''$ rectangles in blue (violet)
51 $2'' \times 3\frac{1}{2}''$ rectangles in silver (gold)
23 $1\frac{1}{2}'' \times 2\frac{3}{4}''$ rectangles in yellow (for belly)
12 $\frac{3}{4}'' \times 1\frac{1}{2}''$ rectangles in gold (silver)
 1 $2'' \times 3\frac{1}{2}''$ rectangle in red

Fold into type C triangles (see page 26).

Other materials per dragon

6″ thick gold string
34″ thin gold string
1 miniature bell
2 ¼″ plastic eyes
Cardboard

❶

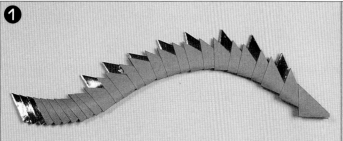

Make beam A that forms the "backbone". Join 35 triangles changing color referring to the diagram on the opposite page, and shaping as shown on page 30. Glue each piece as you join.

❷

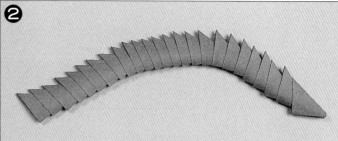

Make 2 of beam B to form the sides: Join 25 triangles shaping in the same manner as beam A. Glue each piece as you join.

❸

Make 2 of beam C to form streaks. Join 17 metallic color pieces shaping in the same manner.

❹

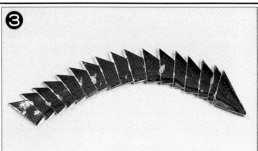

●See page 30.

Make neck by joining 19 pieces referring to the diagram. Glue each piece and attach eyes, bell and cut strings with glue.

❺

Glue 5 rows of body, shaping carefully.

❻

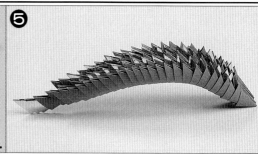

●See page 30.

Paste a gold rectangle onto cardboard. Copy the hind foot shape and cut out.

❼

●See page 30.

Make belly by joining 23 pieces, and glue onto the body, shaping alike.

❽

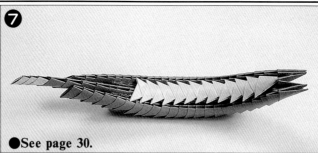

Make forefeet according to the diagram.

❾

Glue on fore and hind feet. Trim the tail as shown on page 30.

❿

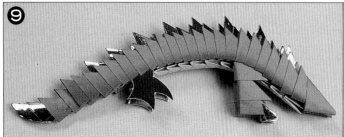

Attach neck and head for completed dragon.

28   **Note:** Completed project may look different depending on the thickness of paper used.

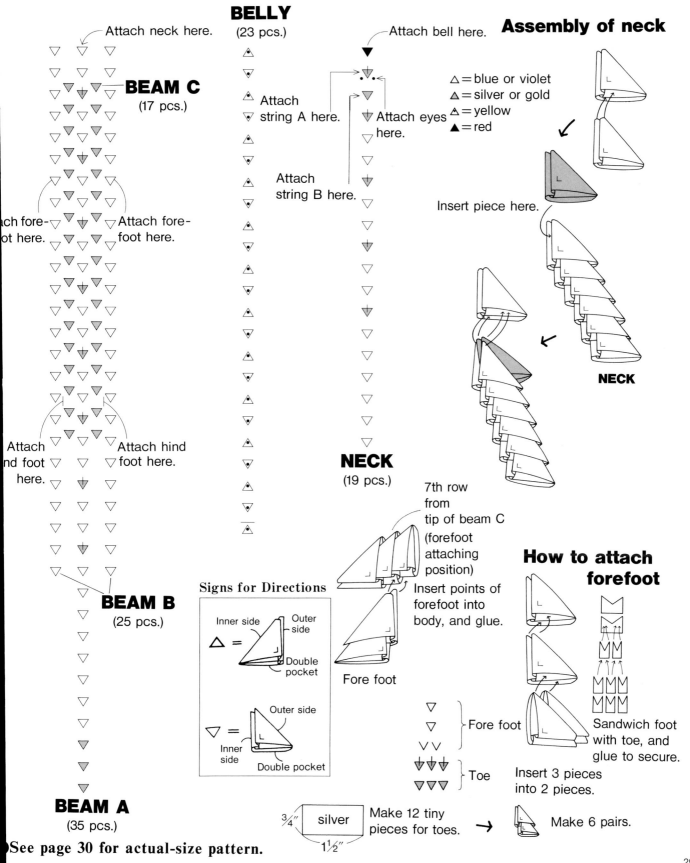

BELLY
(23 pcs.)

Attach neck here.

Attach bell here.

BEAM C
(17 pcs.)

Assembly of neck

Attach string A here.

△ = blue or violet
△ = silver or gold
△ = yellow
▲ = red

Attach eyes here.

Attach string B here.

Insert piece here.

ch fore-ot here.

Attach fore-foot here.

NECK

Attach nd foot here.

Attach hind foot here.

NECK
(19 pcs.)

7th row from tip of beam C (forefoot attaching position)

Insert points of forefoot into body, and glue.

How to attach forefoot

BEAM B
(25 pcs.)

Signs for Directions

Inner side | Outer side

△ =

Double pocket

Outer side

▽ =

Inner side | Double pocket

Fore foot

Fore foot

Toe

Sandwich foot with toe, and glue to secure.

Insert 3 pieces into 2 pieces.

BEAM A
(35 pcs.)

3/4″ | silver | Make 12 tiny pieces for toes.
1½″

→ Make 6 pairs.

◗See page 30 for actual-size pattern.

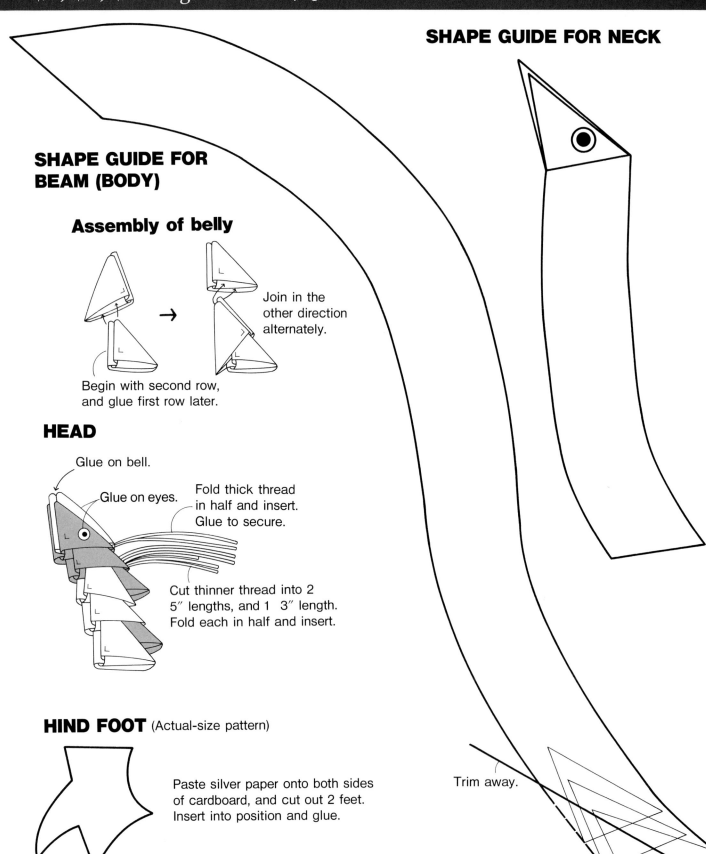

SHAPE GUIDE FOR NECK

SHAPE GUIDE FOR BEAM (BODY)

Assembly of belly

Join in the other direction alternately.

Begin with second row, and glue first row later.

HEAD

Glue on bell.

Glue on eyes.

Fold thick thread in half and insert. Glue to secure.

Cut thinner thread into 2 5″ lengths, and 1 3″ length. Fold each in half and insert.

HIND FOOT (Actual-size pattern)

Paste silver paper onto both sides of cardboard, and cut out 2 feet. Insert into position and glue.

Trim away.

#1, #2 Piggyback Turtles shown on page 4

Paper materials
(all 2″×3½″ craft paper)
- 112 rectangles in red (black)
- 35 rectangles in gold
- 16 rectangles in silver
- 22 rectangles in gray

Fold into type C triangles (see page 26).

Other materials
- 4 ¼″ plastic eyes

◆ #2 is a black version of #1.

Finished size
Adult turtle: 5″×6½″
Baby turtle: 3½″×5″

ADULT TURTLE

▽ ·························· Row 15 (1 pc.)
▽ ▽ ···················· Row 14 (2 pcs.)
▽ ▼ ▽ ················· Row 13 (3 pcs.)
▽ ▼ ▼ ▽ ·············· Row 12 (4 pcs.)
▽ ▼ ▼ ▼ ▽ ··········· Row 11 (5 pcs.)
▽ ▼ ▽ ▽ ▼ ▽ ········ Row 10 (6 pcs.)
▽ ▼ ▽ ▼ ▽ ▼ ▽ ····· Row 9 (7 pcs.)
▽ ▼ ▽ ▽ ▽ ▽ ▼ ▽ ·· Row 8 (8 pcs.)
▽ ▼ ▽ ▽ ▽ ▽ ▼ ▽ Row 7 (9 pcs.)
▽ ▼ ▽ ▽ ▽ ▽ ▽ ▼ ▽ Row 6 (10 pcs.)
▽ ▼ ▽ ▽ ▽ ▽ ▽ ▼ ▽ Row 5 (11 pcs.)
▽ ▼ ▽ ▽ ▽ ▽ ▽ ▽ ▼ ▽ Row 4 (12 pcs.)
▽ ▼ ▽ ▽ ▽ ▽ ▽ ▽ ▽ ▼ ▽ Row 3 (13 pcs.)
▽ ▽ ▽ ▽ ▽ ▽ ▽ ▽ ▽ ▽ ▽ ▽ ▽ Row 2 (13 pcs.)
△ △ △ △ △ △ △ △ △ △ △ △ △ Row 1 (13 pcs.)

△ = red
△ = gray
▲ = gold
△ = silver

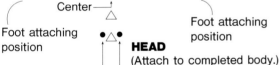

Center
Foot attaching position
Foot attaching position
HEAD (Attach to completed body.)
Eye attaching position

BABY TURTLE

▽ ················· Row 11 (1 pc.)
▽ ▽ ············· Row 10 (2 pcs.)
▽ ▼ ▽ ·········· Row 9 (3 pcs.)
▽ ▼ ▼ ▽ ······· Row 8 (4 pcs.)
▽ ▼ ▽ ▼ ▽ ···· Row 7 (5 pcs.)
▽ ▼ ▽ ▼ ▽ Row 6 (6 pcs.)
▽ ▼ ▽ ▽ ▼ ▽ Row 5 (7 pcs.)
▽ ▼ ▽ ▽ ▼ ▽ Row 4 (8 pcs.)
▽ ▼ ▽ ▽ ▼ ▼ ▽ Row 3 (9 pcs.)
▽ ▽ ▽ ▽ ▽ ▽ ▽ ▽ ▽ Row 2 (9 pcs.)
△ △ △ △ △ △ △ △ △ Row 1 (9 pcs.)

Center
HEAD (Attach to completed body.)
Eye attaching position

FOOT (for ADULT TURTLE)

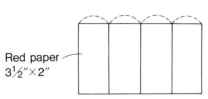

Red paper 3½″×2″

Cut into quarters and fold each into triangle.

↓

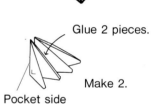

Glue 2 pieces.

Make 2.

Pocket side

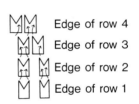

Edge of row 4
Edge of row 3
Edge of row 2
Edge of row 1

↓

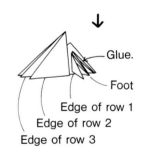

Glue.
Foot
Edge of row 1
Edge of row 2
Edge of row 3

Signs for Directions

Inner side — Outer side
△ =
Double pocket

Outer side
▽ =
Inner side
Double pocket

Edge of row 4
Edge of row 3
Edge of row 2
Edge of row 1

HEAD

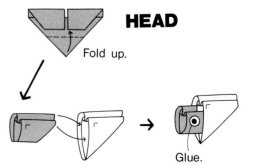

Fold up.

→

Glue.

#8, #9 Long Life Turtle shown on page 10

Paper materials per turtle (craft paper)

12	$\frac{1}{4}'' \times 4''$ rectangles in gold (paw base)
147	$1\frac{1}{2} \times 2\frac{1}{2}''$ rectangles in gold (shell, sides, tail)
80	$\frac{3}{4}'' \times 2\frac{1}{2}''$ rectangles in gold (claw)
188	$1\frac{1}{2}'' \times 2\frac{1}{2}''$ rectangles in silver or pink (shell, tail)
32	$\frac{3}{4}'' \times 2''$ rectangles in silver or pink (claw)
170	$1\frac{1}{2}'' \times 2\frac{1}{2}''$ rectangles in cream (belly, feet)

Fold into type C triangles (see page 26.) except claws.

Other materials per turtle

1   styrofoam turtle head in gold
2   $\frac{1}{4}''$ plastic eyes

Finished size: $5\frac{1}{2}'' \times 9''$

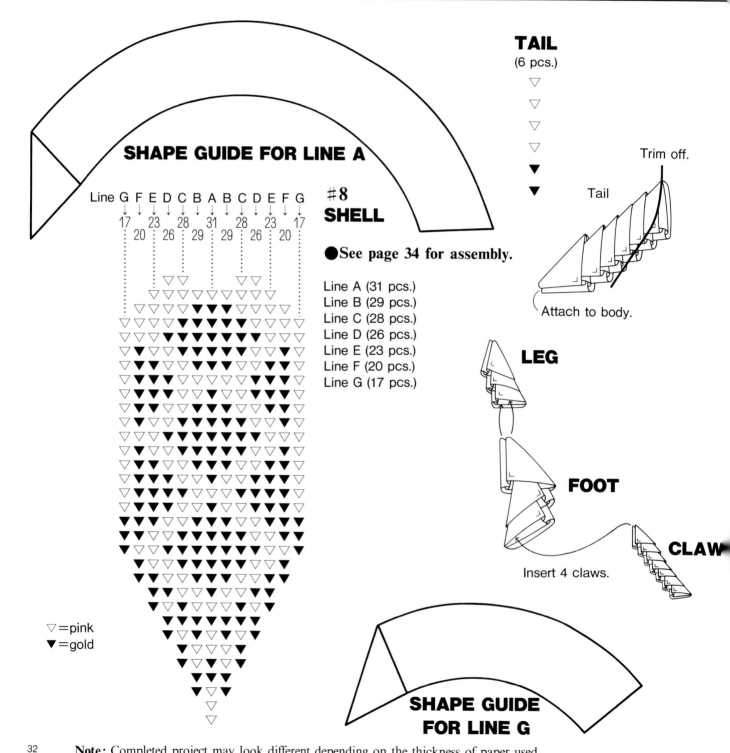

SHAPE GUIDE FOR LINE A

Line G F E D C B A B C D E F G
17   23   28   31   28   23   17
  20   26   29   29   26   20

#8 SHELL

●See page 34 for assembly.

Line A (31 pcs.)
Line B (29 pcs.)
Line C (28 pcs.)
Line D (26 pcs.)
Line E (23 pcs.)
Line F (20 pcs.)
Line G (17 pcs.)

▽=pink
▼=gold

TAIL
(6 pcs.)

Trim off.

Tail

Attach to body.

LEG

FOOT

CLAW

Insert 4 claws.

SHAPE GUIDE FOR LINE G

32   **Note:** Completed project may look different depending on the thickness of paper used.

LEG (10 pcs.)
Shape in the same manner as shell.

△=gold
▲=silver
▽=cream

▽ } Paw base
▽ } (Use 2¼″×4″ rectangles.)

Claw (Use ¾″×2″ rectangles.)

Signs for Directions

△ = Inner side / Outer side / Double pocket

▽ = Outer side / Inner side / Double pocket

BELLY

△△△△△△△△△ ·········· Row 12 (8 pcs.)
△△△△△△△△△△ ········ Row 11 (10 pcs.)
△△△△△△△△△△△ ······ Row 10 (11 pcs.)
△△△△△△△△△△△△ ····· Row 9 (12 pcs.)
△△△△△△△△△△△△△ ···· Row 8 (13 pcs.)
△△△△△△△△△△△△△ ··· Row 7 (13 pcs.)
△△△△△△△△△△△△△ ···· Row 6 (13 pcs.)
△△△△△△△△△△△△ ····· Row 5 (12 pcs.)
△△△△△△△△△△△ ······ Row 4 (11 pcs.)
△△△△△△△△△△ ········ Row 3 (10 pcs.)
△△△△△△△△△ ·········· Row 2 (9 pcs.)
△△△△△△△△ ··········· Row 1 (8 pcs.)

#9 SHELL

Line A (29 pcs.)
Line B (28 pcs.)
Line C (30 pcs.)
Line D (25 pcs.)
Line E (22 pcs.)
Line F (19 pcs.)
Line G (16 pcs.)

Line G F E D C B A B C D E F G

Start by making Line A. Make Lines B to G, and glue to Line A in order, slightly lower than the previous line. Glue gun is recommended for this purpose.

How to decrease at sides

How to increase at sides

Tail attaching position

▽=silver
▼=gold

SIDE
(Use 10 pcs.)

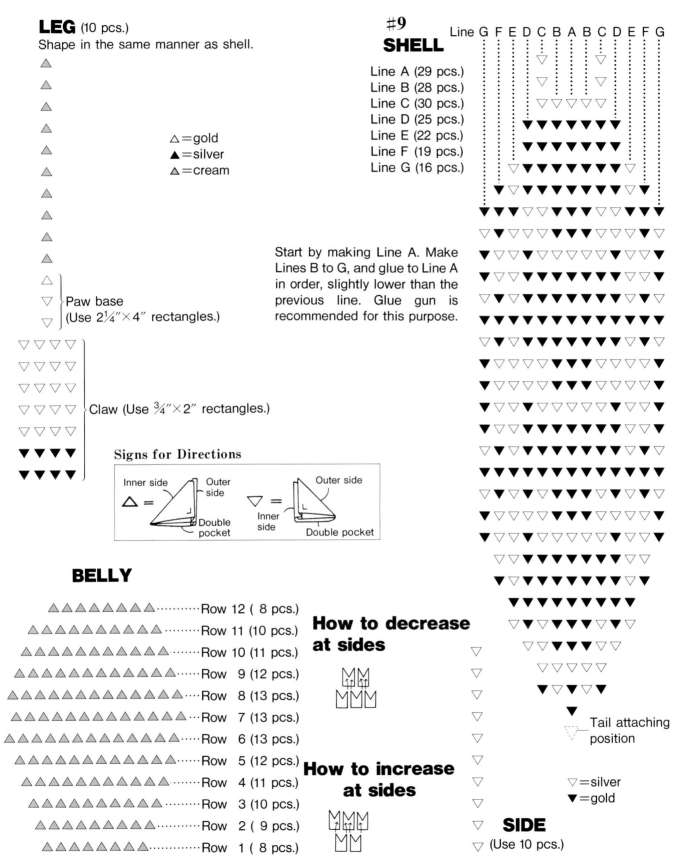

①

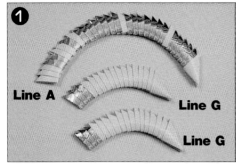

Line A

Line G

Line G

Assemble each line according to the color chart (previous page), and glue to keep the arch shape. See above to check the contrast between Line A and Line G.

②

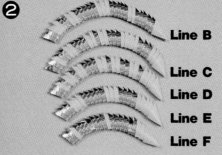

Line B

Line C

Line D

Line E

Line F

Make all remaining rows from B to F according to the color chart, but do not apply glue.

③

Glue each row onto the sides of Line A in order, slightly lower than the previous line so that a dome shape is achieved.

④

13 beams are stuck together, forming a dome.

⑤

Using the smallest pieces, make claws and glue together. Make 16 claws, 4 for each leg.

⑥

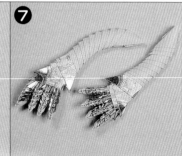

Make 4 feet, gluing 3 largest pieces each.

⑦

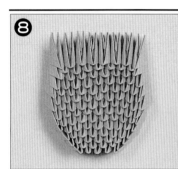

Into the pocket side of foot, insert 4 claws. Join 10 pieces of leg, gluing together.

⑧

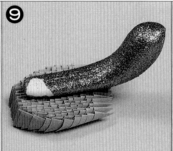

Assemble belly using a light color pieces, referring to the diagram on page 33.

⑨

Glue on turtle turtle head so that the end is slightly inside belly.

⑩

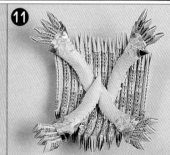

Make side beams using 10 pieces as shown.

⑪

Glue legs onto the underside of shell, overlapping ends.

⑫

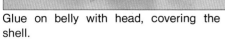

Glue on belly with head, covering the shell.

⑬

Add side beams. Attach tail.

⑭

Attach eyes for completed turtle.

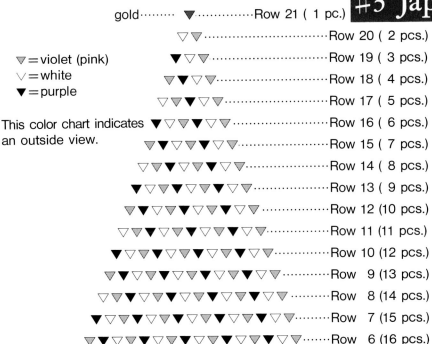

gold ········ ▼ ·············· Row 21 (1 pc.)

▽▼ ·························· Row 20 (2 pcs.)

▽ = violet (pink)
∨ = white
▼ = purple

▼ ▽▼ ························· Row 19 (3 pcs.)

▼ ▽ ▽▼ ······················ Row 18 (4 pcs.)

This color chart indicates
an outside view.

▽ ▼ ▽ ▼▽ ················· Row 17 (5 pcs.)

▼ ▽ ▼ ▼ ▽ ▼ ············ Row 16 (6 pcs.)

▽ ▼ ▽ ▼ ▼ ▽ ▼ ········ Row 15 (7 pcs.)

▽ ▼ ▽ ▼ ▽ ▼ ▽ ▼ ····· Row 14 (8 pcs.)

▼ ▽ ▼ ▽ ▼ ▽ ▼ ▽ ▼ ·· Row 13 (9 pcs.)

▽ ▼ ▽ ▼ ▽ ▼ ▼ ▽ ▼ ▽ Row 12 (10 pcs.)

▽ ▽ ▼ ▽ ▼ ▽ ▼ ▽ ▼ ▽ ▼ Row 11 (11 pcs.)

▼ ▽ ▼ ▽ ▼ ▽ ▼ ▽ ▼ ▽ ▼ ▽ Row 10 (12 pcs.)

▽ ▼ ▽ ▼ ▽ ▼ ▼ ▽ ▼ ▽ ▼ ▽ ▼ Row 9 (13 pcs.)

▽ ▼ ▽ ▼ ▼ ▽ ▼ ▽ ▼ ▽ ▼ ▽ ▼ ▽ Row 8 (14 pcs.)

▼ ▽ ▼ ▽ ▼ ▽ ▼ ▽ ▼ ▽ ▼ ▽ ▼ ▽ ▼ Row 7 (15 pcs.)

▽ ▼ ▽ ▼ ▽ ▼ ▽ ▼ ▽ ▼ ▽ ▼ ▽ ▼ ▽ ▼ Row 6 (16 pcs.)

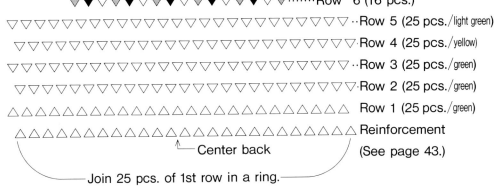

▽▽▽▽▽▽▽▽▽▽▽▽▽▽▽▽▽▽▽▽▽▽▽▽▽ ·· Row 5 (25 pcs./light green)

▽▽▽▽▽▽▽▽▽▽▽▽▽▽▽▽▽▽▽▽▽▽▽▽▽ ·Row 4 (25 pcs./yellow)

▽▽▽▽▽▽▽▽▽▽▽▽▽▽▽▽▽▽▽▽▽▽▽▽▽ ·· Row 3 (25 pcs./green)

▽▽▽▽▽▽▽▽▽▽▽▽▽▽▽▽▽▽▽▽▽▽▽▽▽ ·Row 2 (25 pcs./green)

△△△△△△△△△△△△△△△△△△△△△△△△△ Row 1 (25 pcs./green)

△△△△△△△△△△△△△△△△△△△△△△△△△ Reinforcement

⌐ Center back   (See page 43.)

— Join 25 pcs. of 1st row in a ring.—

Paper materials per doll
(all 1½″×3″ origami cut in half)

1	rectangle in gold
45	rectangles in white
50	rectangles in violet (pink)
40	rectangles in purple (red)
25	rectangles in light green
100	rectangles in green
25	rectangles in yellow

Fold into type A triangles (see page 25).

Other materials per doll
1 2″×3½″ rectangles in black for hair
1 1⅛″ square in gold for headpiece
¾″ wooden bead for doll head

Finished size: 3¼″×5″

ORIGAMI CRANE (headpiece)

① Plain side 1⅛″ 1⅛″ Fold in half.
② Fold in half again.
③
④ Spread out from inside and press down into squares.
⑤ Make creases.
⑥ Turn over and repeat.
⑦ Fold to meet at center.
⑧ Spread, fold up, and press down.
⑨ Finished crane

EMPEROR'S CREST

1⅛″
3/8″
Roll up.
¼″
1⅛″
1/12″ ½″

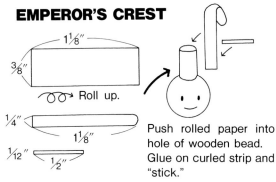

Push rolled paper into hole of wooden bead. Glue on curled strip and "stick."

EMPRESS'S HEADPIECE

Cover the hole of wooden bead with "hair," and attach golden crane.

HAIR (Actual-size pattern)

Note: Completed project may look different depending on the thickness of paper used.

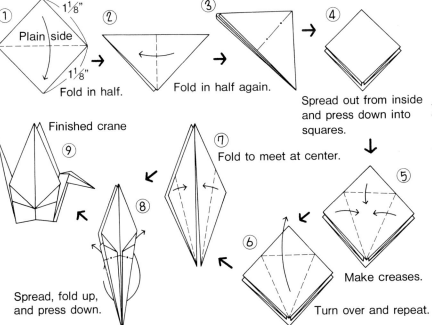

Paper materials (stiff paper in red)
- 65 2″×3½″ rectangles for body
- 4 1¼″×2¼″ rectangles for long feelers
- 6 1″×1¾″ rectangles for short feeler/eye bases/spines

Fold into type C triangles (see page 26).
- 6 ⅜″×3½″ rectangles for long feelers and legs

Other materials
- 2 ⅛″ plastic eyes
- 3 #28 wrapped wire, each 7″ long, 14″ in all

Finished size: 2¼″×9″

BODY

●See page 37 for folding instructions.

Tail {
▽▽ ········ Glue 2 pieces on 18th row.
▽ ········ Row 18 (1 pc.)

△△ ········ Row 17 (2 pcs.)
△△△ ······ Row 16 (3 pcs.)
△△ ········ Row 15 (2 pcs.)
△△△ ······ Row 14 (3 pcs.)
△△ ········ Row 13 (2 pcs.)
△△△ ······ Row 12 (3 pcs.)
△△△△ ····· Row 11 (4 pcs.)
△△△ ······ Row 10 (3 pcs.)

Glue on legs between 5th and 6th rows.
△△△△ ····· Row 9 (4 pcs.)
△△△△△ ··· Row 8 (5 pcs.)
△△△△△△ ·· Row 7 (6 pcs.)

Leg attaching position
△△△△△ ···· Row 6 (5 pcs.)
△△△△△△ ·· Row 5 (6 pcs.)

Spine attaching position
△△△△△ ···· Row 4 (5 pcs.)
△△△△ ····· Row 3 (4 pcs.)

HEAD

△△△ ······ Row 2 (3 pcs.)
△△ ········ Row 1 (2 pcs.)

Eye attaching position

△△
△△ } Join after body is assembled.
△△

Long feeler attaching position

How to assemble

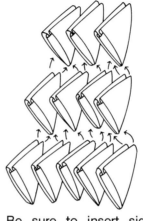

Be sure to insert side flaps for a smooth finish.

Long feeler

Each piece is made of 1″×1¾″ rectangle.

1¼″×2¼″ rectangle

Row 1 of head

Insert and glue.

Short feeler

Feeler attaching position

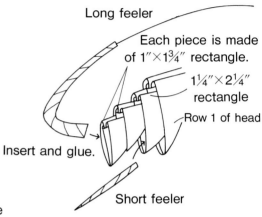

Eye attaching position

Glue on eyes.

Make a triangle from 1″×1¾″ rectangles. Make 2. Insert into center of second row.

Row 2
Row 1

How to make tail

Glue between pieces of 18th row.

Row 18
Row 17

LEG

Wind ⅜″ wide strips of paper around wire at a slant, and glue.

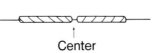

¾″   ¾″

4¾″ Wrapped wire

Glue onto backside of body and bend to shape leg.

↑ Center

→

LONG FEELER

●See page 37 for folding instructions.

With ⅜″ wide strips of paper, wrap wire at a slant into cone, starting with ¼″ diameter.

2¾″

10″ Wrapped wire

↓

Note: Completed project may look different depending on the thickness of paper used.

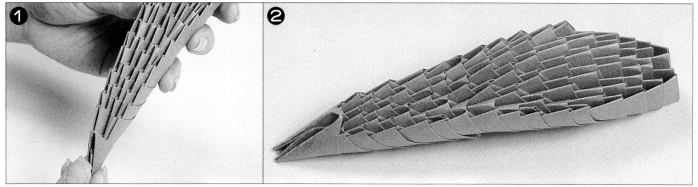

① Assemble body referring to the diagram, from 1st to 17th row. Make tail pieces as shown on the bottom of this page. Join one in opposite direction (Row 18).

② When 18th row is joined, trunk of the body is completed.

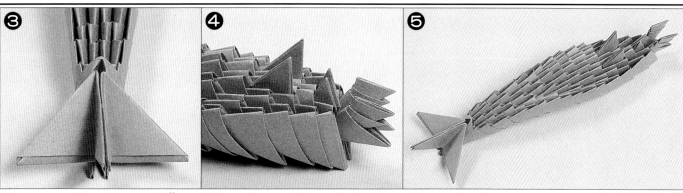

③ Glue on remaining pieces as tail.

④ Make spines and bases for feelers and eyes. Insert a pair of smallest triangles into each position.

⑤ Completed body.

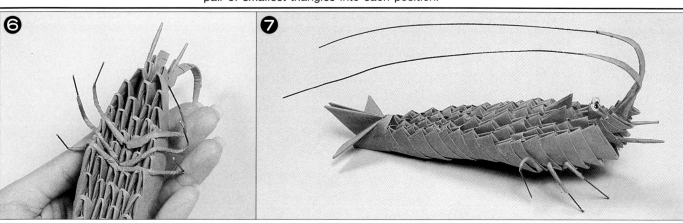

⑥ Glue legs onto backside.

⑦ Attach eyes. Attach long and short feelers by inserting into the bases.

TAIL (Make 3.)

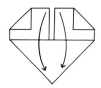

Work as for type C triangle, Step 8, on page 26.

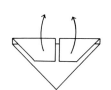

Unfold.

Fold down and tuck in.

Fold in half.

FEELER

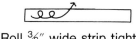

Roll ⅜″ wide strip tightly at a slant; glue.

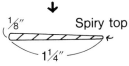

⅛″   Spiry top

1¼″

37

#13, #14 Treasure Boat with Seven Deities of Good Luck

Paper materials per boat (stiff craft paper)
- 199 $1\frac{1}{2}'' \times 2\frac{3}{4}''$ rectangles in black (red), for bottom
- 68 $1\frac{1}{2}'' \times 2\frac{3}{4}''$ rectangles in gold, for trim
- 192 $1\frac{1}{2}'' \times 2\frac{3}{4}''$ rectangles in cream (black), for sail
- 30 $1\frac{1}{2}'' \times 2\frac{3}{4}''$ rectangles in black, for pedestal

Fold into type C triangles (see page 26).

Other materials per boat
A miniature doll set of Seven Deities, about 1″ tall
Kanji character sticker
- 1 $2\frac{1}{2}''$ styrofoam ball, halved
- 2 $\frac{1}{2}''$ styrofoam ball

Crepe paper in pink and red to wrap the balls

Finished size: $8\frac{1}{2}'' \times 3\frac{1}{2}''$

Crown jewel attaching position

SAIL

▽▽▽▽▽▽▽▽▽▽▽▽▽▽▽▽▽▽▽▽····Row 22 (20 pcs.)
▽▽▽▽▽▽▽▽▽▽▼▽▽▽▽▽▽▽▽·····Row 21 (19 pcs.)
▽▽▽▼▼▼▼▼▼▼▼▼▼▼▼▼▽▽▽······Row 20 (18 pcs.)
▽▽▽▼▽▽▽▽▽▽▽▽▽▼▽▽▽········Row 19 (17 pcs.)
▽▽▽▼▼▼▼▼▼▼▽▽▽▽·······Row 18 (16 pcs.)
▽▽▽▽▽▽▽▼▽▽▽▽▽▽▽▽·······Row 17 (17 pcs.)
▽▽▽▽▽▼▼▼▼▼▽▽▽▽▽·······Row 16 (16 pcs.)
▽▽▽▽▼▽▽▽▽▽▽▽▽▽▽▽▽·······Row 15 (17 pcs.)
▽▽▽▽▽▽▼▽▽▽▽▽▽▽▽·······Row 14 (15 pcs.)
▽▽▽▼▼▼▼▼▼▼▼▽▽▽▽·······Row 13 (16 pcs.)
▽▽▽▽▽▽▽▽▽▽▽▽▽▽▽·······Row 12 (15 pcs.)
▽▽▽▽▽▽▽▽▽▽▽▽▽▽▽▽·······Row 11 (16 pcs.)
▽▽▽▽▽▽▽▽▽▽▽▽▽▽▽·········Row 10 (15 pcs.)
▽▽▽▽▽▽▽▽▽▽▽▽▽▽▽▽········Row 9 (16 pcs.)

↑ Center back

The *Kanji* character on the sail, 「宝」 (*takara*), means "treasure."

Making platform for deities

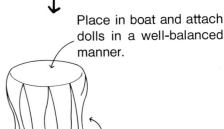

△ = black (red)
▲ = gold
△ = cream (black)

Split larger styrofoam ball in two and use one.

↓

Place in boat and attach dolls in a well-balanced manner.

Cover with pink crepe paper, using glue.

Insert between pieces of previous row.

▼▼
▼▼▼ = (crown shapes)

CROWN JEWEL

Apply glue onto tiny styrofoam and wrap up with red crepe paper.

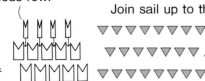

Red crepe paper

Join sail up to this point.

▼···Row 12 (1 pc.)
▼▼···Row 11 (2 pcs.)
▼▽▼···Row 10 (3 pcs.)
▼▽▽▼·····································Row 9 (4 pcs.)

Join sail up to this point.

▽▽▽▽▽▽▽   ▼▽▽▽▼   ▽▽▽▽▽▽▽·····Row 8 (20 pcs.)
▽▽▽▽▽▽▽▽ ▼▽▽▽▽▼ ▽▽▽▽▽▽▽▽····Row 7 (20 pcs.)
▽▽▽▽▽▽▼▼▼▼▼▽▽▽▽▽▼▼▼▼▼▽▽▽▽▽▽····Row 6 (20 pcs.)
▽▽▽▽▽▽▽▽▽▽▽▽▽▽▽▽▽▽▽▽▽▽▽▽▽▽▽▽····Row 5 (28 pcs.)
▽▽▽▽▽▽▽▽▽▽▽▽▽▽▽▽▽▽▽▽▽▽▽▽▽▽▽▽····Row 4 (28 pcs.)
▽▽▽▽▽▽▽▽▽▽▽▽▽▽▽▽▽▽▽▽▽▽▽▽▽▽▽▽····Row 3 (28 pcs.)
▽▽▽▽▽▽▽▽▽▽▽▽▽▽▽▽▽▽▽▽▽▽▽▽▽▽▽▽·····Row 2 (28 pcs.)
△△△△△△△△△△△△△△△△△△△△△△△△△△△△····Row 1 (28 pcs.)

Center back   Center front   Center back

Join 28 pieces in a ring.

▷ ▷

PEDESTAL   Join 30 pieces in a ring of about 2″ inner diameter.

①

Make bottom row. Join 7 triangles, gluing tips together. Make 4 units.

②

Glue and join all units in a ring.

③

Join pieces of 2nd row, reversing the direction, all around.

④

Work in the same manner, using 28 pieces for each round.

⑤

When 5th round is done, start shaping by working 3 more rows only on sail side.

⑥

Shape bow side by working 6th to 10th rows.

⑦
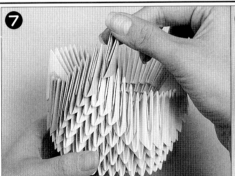
Work another row on the bow side with contrasting color.

⑧
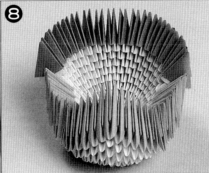
For 7th row of the bow side, insert glued pieces between pieces of previous row.

⑨

Make sail. Referring to the diagram, start from 9th row.

⑩
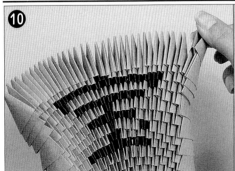
Be sure that pieces are joined evenly as you go. Arrange so that the top line (22nd row) stays neat.

⑪
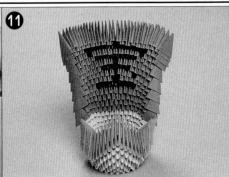
Completed sail. Carefully arrange into a warped shape.

⑫

Glue on platform, dolls and crown jewel for completed treasure boat.

#12 Treasure Boat shown on page 11

Paper materials (all 2″×3½″ craft paper)
365 rectangles in gold for bottom and sail
34 rectangles in black for *kanji* character
Fold into type C triangles (see page 26).
Ornaments

Finished size: 5½″×8″

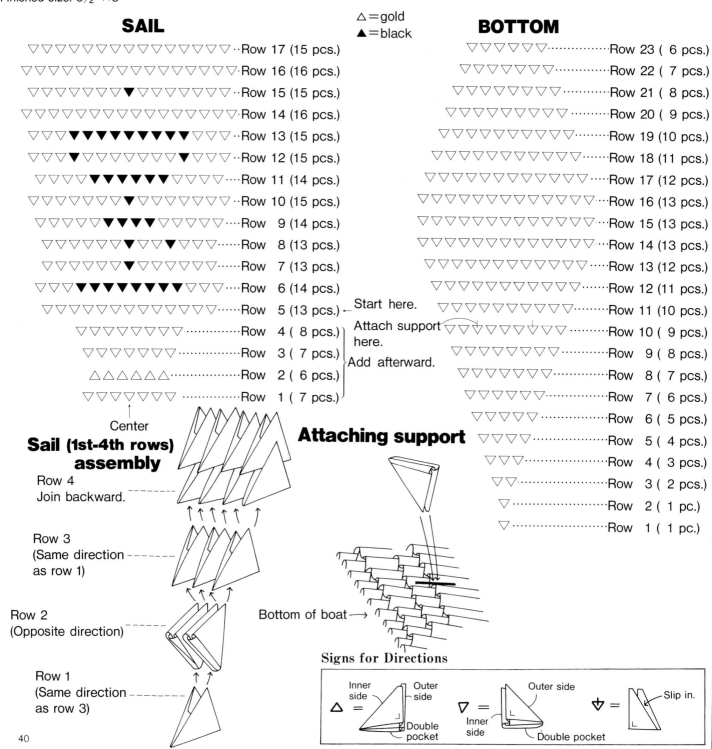

△=gold
▲=black

SAIL

Row 17 (15 pcs.)
Row 16 (16 pcs.)
Row 15 (15 pcs.)
Row 14 (16 pcs.)
Row 13 (15 pcs.)
Row 12 (15 pcs.)
Row 11 (14 pcs.)
Row 10 (15 pcs.)
Row 9 (14 pcs.)
Row 8 (13 pcs.)
Row 7 (13 pcs.)
Row 6 (14 pcs.)
Row 5 (13 pcs.) ← Start here.
Row 4 (8 pcs.)
Row 3 (7 pcs.)
Row 2 (6 pcs.)
Row 1 (7 pcs.)

Attach support here.
Add afterward.

Center

BOTTOM

Row 23 (6 pcs.)
Row 22 (7 pcs.)
Row 21 (8 pcs.)
Row 20 (9 pcs.)
Row 19 (10 pcs.)
Row 18 (11 pcs.)
Row 17 (12 pcs.)
Row 16 (13 pcs.)
Row 15 (13 pcs.)
Row 14 (13 pcs.)
Row 13 (12 pcs.)
Row 12 (11 pcs.)
Row 11 (10 pcs.)
Row 10 (9 pcs.)
Row 9 (8 pcs.)
Row 8 (7 pcs.)
Row 7 (6 pcs.)
Row 6 (5 pcs.)
Row 5 (4 pcs.)
Row 4 (3 pcs.)
Row 3 (2 pcs.)
Row 2 (1 pc.)
Row 1 (1 pc.)

Sail (1st-4th rows) assembly

Row 4
Join backward.

Row 3
(Same direction as row 1)

Row 2
(Opposite direction)

Row 1
(Same direction as row 3)

Attaching support

Bottom of boat →

Signs for Directions

Inner side — Outer side
△ = Double pocket

Outer side
▽ = Inner side — Double pocket

⇩ = Slip in.

❶ Make bottom: Work from 1st to 16th row, increasing pieces as shown in the diagram.

❷ Completed body. The number of pieces is decreased from 17th row.

❸ Insert and glue a pair of support.

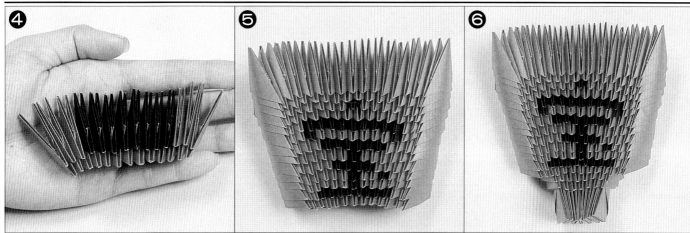

❹ Make sail: Start from 5th row, gluing each piece to secure.

❺ 5th to 17th rows are completed. Be sure to straighten the top line.

❻ Add "base" to bottom (5th row). Add 4th, 3rd, 2nd rows, and then 1st row.

❼ Glue sail onto body.

❽ Attach ornaments as appropriate for completed treasure boat.

#16 Sitting Crane shown on page 12

Paper materials (all 2″×3½″ stiff craft paper)
- 377 rectangles in white
- 52 rectangles in black
- 1 rectangle in red
- 1 rectangle in yellow

Fold into type C triangles (see page 26).

Other materials
- 6″×4″ cardboard
- 2 ¼″ plastic eyes
- 12″ ¼″ gold ribbon

Finished size: 6″×9″

Tips: When all pieces are joined, slot in dab of glue between pieces for a stable project.

△ = white
▲ = black

▼·Row 14 (1 pc.
▼···Row 13 (1 pc.
▼ ▼·Row 12 (2 pcs
▼ ▼···Row 11 (2 pcs
▽ ▽ ▽·Row 10 (3 pcs

Neck attaching position

▼ ▼ ▼···Row 9 (3 pcs
·Row 8 (34 pcs
···Row 7 (34 pcs
·Row 6 (34 pcs
····Row 5 (34 pcs
··Row 4 (51 pcs
·Row 3 (51 pcs
··Row 2 (51 pcs
Row 1 (51 pcs

Reinforcement

Center front

Join 51 pieces of 1st row in a ring.

Decreasing

---- Row 5

---- Row 4

Insert 3 tips into 1 piece, which results in decrease of pieces by stacking 2 pieces over 3 pieces.

NECK (19 pcs.)

yellow → ▽
▽
red → ▲
▽
▽
▽
▽
▽
▼
▼
▽
▽
▽
▽
▽
▽
▽

Yellow

White

Red

NECK (Actual-size curving pattern)

NECK (Actual-size curving pattern)

42   **Note:** Completed project may look different depending on the thickness of paper used.

❶

Join 5 to 6 triangles, gluing tips together. Repeat making the same unit until all 51 triangles are joined.

❷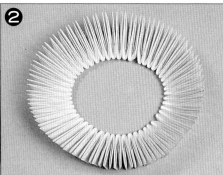

Glue all units to make a ring. This makes 1st row.

❸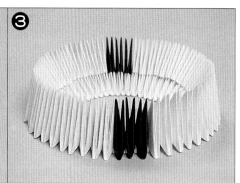

Work 2nd round by inserting pieces in reverse direction. This makes a wider ring.

❹

Turn over and insert 51 pieces into 1st row for reinforcement.

❺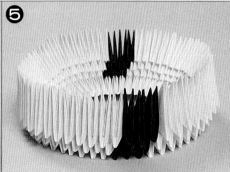

Turn over again, and work 3rd and 4th rounds (51 pieces each) according to the color chart.

❻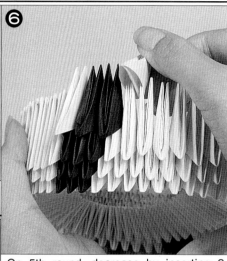

On 5th round, decrease by inserting 3 points into 1 piece of previous row (see opposite page).

❼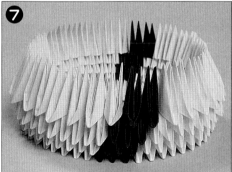

5th round completed with only 34 pieces.

❽

Work the same until 8th round is done.

❾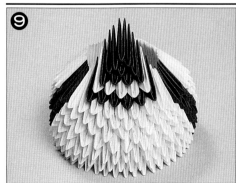

Form tail while working 9th to 14th row, referring to the diagram.

❿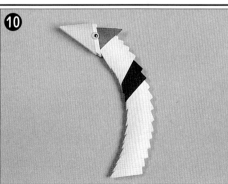

Make neck and head with 19 pieces, and shape according to the guide.

⓫

Attach neck/head in position. Make a ribbon bow and attach at the base of neck. Cut out a circle from cardboard and glue onto bottom.

43

#15 Flopping Crane shown on page 12

Paper materials (origami cut in half)
404 1½″×2¾″ rectangles in gold
1 1½″×2¾″ rectangle in silver
Fold into type A triangles (see page 25).
Other materials
2 ¼″ plastic eyes

◆For the similar project on page 3, use scrap paper (magazine paper), folded into type B triangles.

Note: Completed project may look different depending on the thickness of paper used.

Finished size: 5″×4″

SHAPE GUIDE FOR NECK/HEAD

Pockets

Row 1

↓

Row 1

Pockets

Row 2

Row 3

Row 2

Row 1

On 3rd row, reverse the direction of pieces.

7th row

Attach eyes here.

△ = Gold
▲ = Silver
△ = Use plain side if using colorful scrap paper.

When using colorful scrap paper, use the white side to make neck.

△	Row 20 (2 pcs.)
△△	Row 19 (4 pcs.)
△△△	Row 18 (6 pcs.)
△△△△	Row 17 (8 pcs.)
△△△△△	Row 16 (10 pcs.)
△△△△△△	Row 15 (12 pcs.)
△△△△△△△	Row 14 (14 pcs.)
△△△△△△△△	Row 13 (16 pcs.)
△△△△△△△△△	Row 12 (19 pcs.)
△△△△△△△△△△	Row 11 (22 pcs.)
△△△△△△△△△△△	Row 10 (25 pcs.)
△△△△△△△△△△△△	Row 9 (26 pcs.)
△△△△△△△△△△△△△	Row 8 (27 pcs.)

Attach neck here.

Row 7 (same)
Row 6 (same)
Row 5 (same)
Row 4 (same)
Row 3 (same)
Row 2 (same as below)
Row 1 (28 pcs.)

Change the piece direction here (see peag 46).

Center back
Join 28 pieces in a ring.

① Holding 2 pieces pocket side down, insert their 2 center peaks into a piece of 2nd row.

② Add another piece, joining adjacent peaks with a 2nd row piece. Glue each piece.

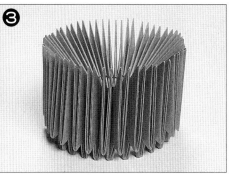

③ Repeat until 28 pieces are joined in a ring forming rows 1-2.

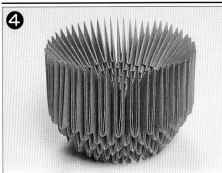

④ Work 3rd to 7th row joining 28 pieces on each row.

⑤ Reverse the direction of pieces on 8th row and onward.

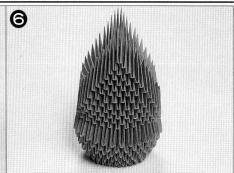

⑥ Form wings by working 8th to 20th row.

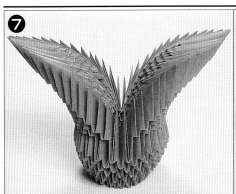

⑦ Completed wings.

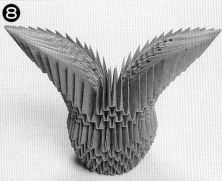

⑧ Form tail according to the diagram.

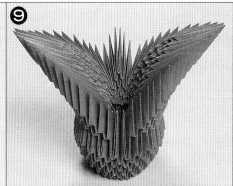

⑨ Front view of completed wings and tail.

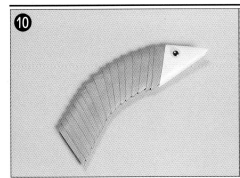

⑩ Make neck and head by gluing 18 pieces into shape. Attach eyes.

⑪ Make pedestal. Join and glue 20-25 pieces in a ring, adjusting to the size of bird.

⑫ Attach neck/head and pedestal for completed crane.

Paper materials (thick craft paper)

#17: 259 ¾″×1½″ rectangles in pink (body)
12 ¾″×1½″ rectangles in black (body)
21 ½″×1⅛″ rectangles in pink (neck)
1 ½″×1⅛″ rectangle in black (head)
1 ⅜″×2¼″ rectangle in black (beak)

#18 : 259 1½″×3¼″ rectangles in white (body)

12 1½″×3¼″ rectangles in black (body)
18 1⅛″×2¼″ rectangles in white (neck)
1 1⅛″×2¼″ rectangle in black (head)
1 ¾″×3½″ rectangle in black (beak)

Fold into triangles(see opposite page) excluding one for "beak".

Other materials
Gold string

Finished size: #17 : 3″×2¼″
#18 : 6½″×4½″

Note: Completed project may look different depending on the thickness of paper used

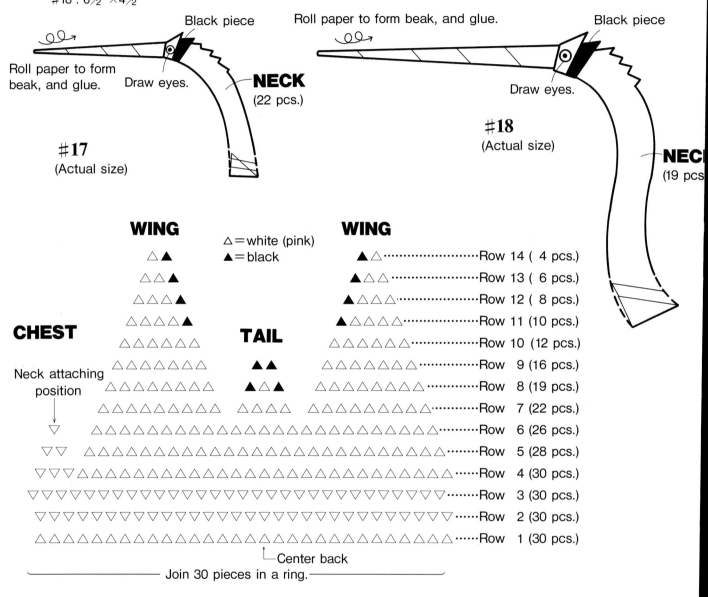

Roll paper to form beak, and glue.

Black piece

Roll paper to form beak, and glue.

Black piece

Draw eyes.

NECK
(22 pcs.)

Draw eyes.

#18
(Actual size)

#17
(Actual size)

NECK
(19 pcs.)

WING

△ = white (pink)
▲ = black

△ ▲
△ △ ▲
△ △ △ ▲
△ △ △ △ ▲

CHEST

△ △ △ △ △ △
△ △ △ △ △ △ △

Neck attaching
position

△ △ △ △ △ △ △ △
▽
▽ ▽
▽ ▽ ▽
▽ ▽ ▽ ▽ ▽
▽ ▽ ▽ ▽ ▽ ▽ ▽ ▽
△ △ △ △ △ △ △ △ △ △ △

TAIL

▲ ▲
▲ △ ▲

△ △ △ △

WING

▲ △ ·············· Row 14 (4 pcs.)
▲ △ △ ·············· Row 13 (6 pcs.)
▲ △ △ △ ·············· Row 12 (8 pcs.)
▲ △ △ △ △ ·············· Row 11 (10 pcs.)
△ △ △ △ △ △ ·············· Row 10 (12 pcs.)
△ △ △ △ △ △ ·············· Row 9 (16 pcs.)
△ △ △ △ △ △ △ ·············· Row 8 (19 pcs.)
△ △ △ △ △ △ △ △ ·············· Row 7 (22 pcs.)
△ △ △ △ △ △ △ △ △ △ ·············· Row 6 (26 pcs.)
△ △ △ △ △ △ △ △ △ △ △ △ △ △ ·············· Row 5 (28 pcs.)
△ △ △ △ △ △ △ △ △ △ △ △ △ △ △ ·············· Row 4 (30 pcs.)
▽ ▽ ▽ ▽ ▽ ▽ ▽ ▽ ▽ ▽ ▽ ▽ ▽ ▽ ▽ ▽ ▽ ·············· Row 3 (30 pcs.)
▽ ▽ ▽ ▽ ▽ ▽ ▽ ▽ ▽ ▽ ▽ ▽ ▽ ▽ ▽ ▽ ▽ ·············· Row 2 (30 pcs.)
△ △ △ △ △ △ △ △ △ △ △ △ △ △ △ △ △ △ △ ·············· Row 1 (30 pcs.)

└ Center back

── Join 30 pieces in a ring. ──

Signs for Directions

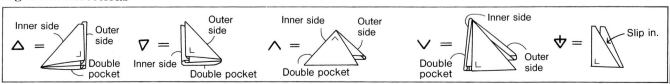

△ = Inner side / Outer side / Double pocket

▽ = Inner side / Outer side / Double pocket / Inner side

∧ = Inner side / Outer side / Double pocket

∨ = Inner side / Double pocket / Outer side

⩔ = Inner side / Slip in.

#20 Swan shown on page 13

Paper materials (thick craft paper)

- 271 ¾″×1½″ rectangles in white
- 4 ¾″×1½″ rectangles in green
- 1 ¾″×1½″ rectangle in yellow
- 1 ⅜″×2¼″ rectangle in orange

Note: Completed project may look different depending on the thickness of paper used.

HOW TO FOLD INTO TRIANGLES FOR PROJECTS #17, #18, #19 and #20

① Fold in half.

② Fold in half again.

③ Fold up diagonally. Turn over and repeat.

④ Unfold.

⑤ Fold up diagonally.

⑥ ←Leave no space.

⑦ Fold in half. ← Leave no space.

⑧ Finished piece
Pocket→ side

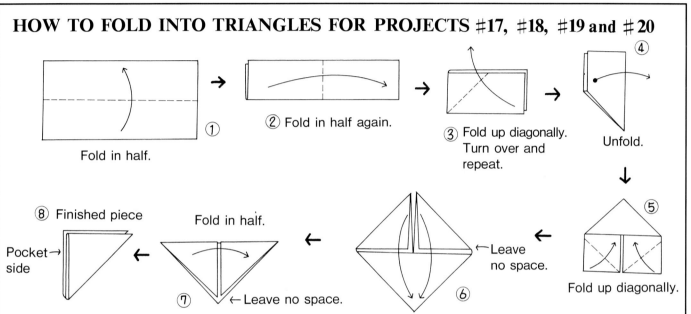

Roll paper to form beak, and glue.

▽ = white
▼ = green

		WING					WING				

WING ▽ ▼   **WING** ▼ ▽ ·········· Row 13 (4 pcs.)

▽ ▽ ▽   ▽ ▽ ▽ ·········· Row 12 (6 pcs.)

▽ ▽ ▽ ▽   ▽ ▽ ▽ ▽ ·········· Row 11 (8 pcs.)

CHEST   Neck   ▽ ▽ ▽ ▽ ▽   **TAIL**   ▽ ▽ ▽ ▽ ▽ ·········· Row 10 (10 pcs.)

attaching ▽ ▽ ▽ ▽ ▽ ▽   ▽ ▽ ▽ ▽ ▽ ▽ ·········· Row 9 (16 pcs.)

position ▽ ▽ ▽   ▽ ▽ ▽ ▽ ▽ ▽ ▽   ▼ ▼   ▽ ▽ ▽   ▽ ▽ ▽ ▽ ▽ ▽ ▽ ·········· Row 8 (20 pcs.)

▽ ▽ ▽ ▽   ▽ ▽ ▽ ▽ ▽ ▽ ▽ ▽   ▽ ▽ ▽   ▽ ▽ ▽ ▽ ▽ ▽ ▽ ▽ ·········· Row 7 (24 pcs.)

▽ ▽ ▽ ▽ ▽   ▽ ▽ ▽ ▽ ▽ ▽ ▽ ▽ ▽   ▽ ▽ ▽ ▽ ▽ ▽ ▽ ▽ ▽ ▽ ·········· Row 6 (28 pcs.)

▽ ·········· Row 5 (30 pcs.)

▽ ·········· Row 4 (30 pcs.)

▽ ·········· Row 3 (30 pcs.)

▽ ·········· Row 2 (30 pcs.)

△ ·········· Row 1 (30 pcs.)

Center front   Center back

Join 30 pieces in a ring.

Orange   Yellow

Draw eyes.

NECK (10 pcs.)
(Actual size)

#19 Chicken shown on page 13

Paper materials (stiff craft paper)
- 299 ¾″×1½″ rectangles in white
- 1 ½″×1¾″ rectangle in yellow
- 3 ½″×1⅛″ rectangle in red
- 1 ⅜″×2¼″ rectangle in orange for beak

Fold into triangles (see page 47).

Note: Completed project may look different depending on the thickness of paper used.

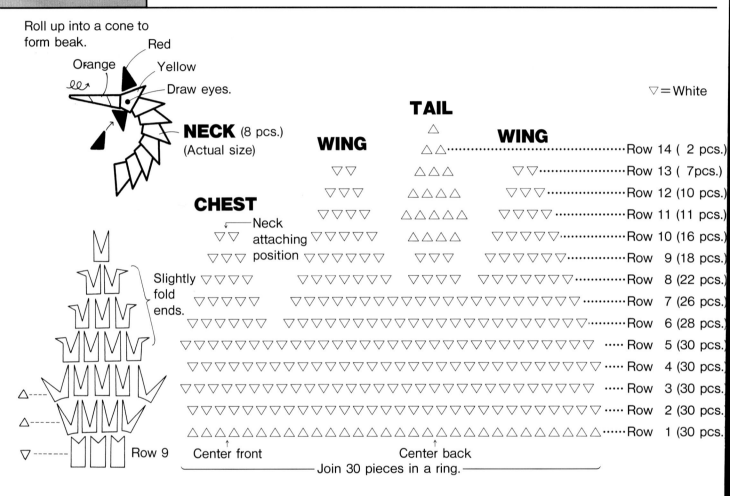

Roll up into a cone to form beak.

Orange
Red
Yellow
Draw eyes.

▽ = White

NECK (8 pcs.)
(Actual size)

TAIL

WING

WING

CHEST

Neck attaching position

Slightly fold ends.

Row 9

Center front

Center back

Join 30 pieces in a ring.

- Row 14 (2 pcs.)
- Row 13 (7pcs.)
- Row 12 (10 pcs.)
- Row 11 (11 pcs.)
- Row 10 (16 pcs.)
- Row 9 (18 pcs.)
- Row 8 (22 pcs.)
- Row 7 (26 pcs.)
- Row 6 (28 pcs.)
- Row 5 (30 pcs.)
- Row 4 (30 pcs.)
- Row 3 (30 pcs.)
- Row 2 (30 pcs.)
- Row 1 (30 pcs.)

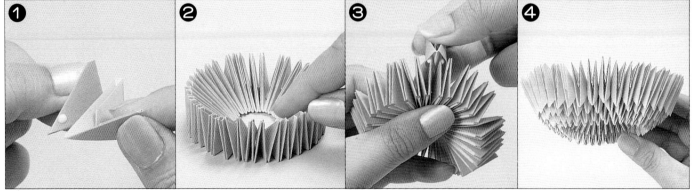

❶ Take 6 to 7 pieces. Apply glue to tip of each piece and join. Make the same unit until 39 pieces are used.

❷ Join all units with glue, forming a ring.

❸ Turn over and work 2nd row, by inserting peaks of previous row into pockets. Repeat until 4th round is done.

❹ Be sure to change colors according to the diagram.

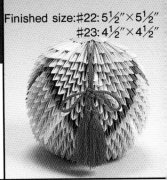

Finished size: #22: 5½″×5½″
#23: 4½″×4½″

#22, #23 Traditional Japanese Hand Ball shown on page 14

Paper materials (all 1¼″×2¼″ thin craft paper)
   72   rectangles in white
   75   rectangles in yellow
   75   rectangles in blue
   617 rectangles in red gradation
Fold into type C triangles (see page 26), saveing 2 pieces of red gradation for covering top and bottom.

Other materials per ball
   Japanese cord with decorative bow
   Japanese bell

◆ **#22** is a scrap paper version made of 1½″× 2¾″ rectangles.

▼ = blue   ▽ = yellow   △▽ = red gradation   ▼ = white

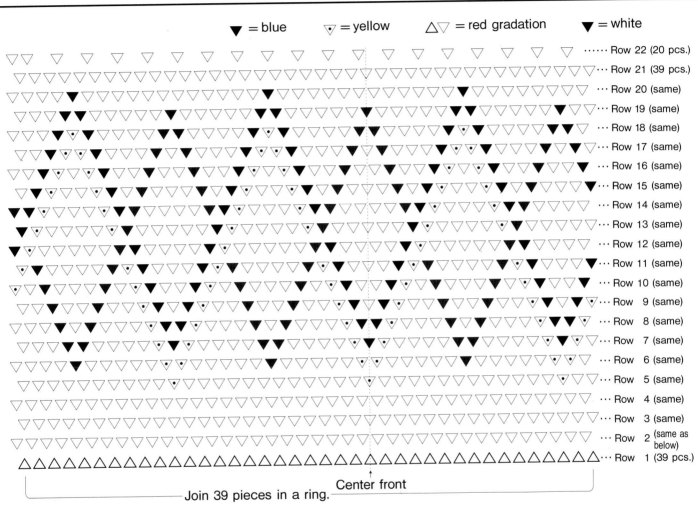

······ Row 22 (20 pcs.)
··· Row 21 (39 pcs.)
··· Row 20 (same)
··· Row 19 (same)
··· Row 18 (same)
··· Row 17 (same)
··· Row 16 (same)
··· Row 15 (same)
··· Row 14 (same)
··· Row 13 (same)
··· Row 12 (same)
··· Row 11 (same)
··· Row 10 (same)
··· Row 9 (same)
··· Row 8 (same)
··· Row 7 (same)
··· Row 6 (same)
··· Row 5 (same)
··· Row 4 (same)
··· Row 3 (same)
··· Row 2 (same as below)
··· Row 1 (39 pcs.)

Center front

Join 39 pieces in a ring.

❺ Work carefully with color pattern until 20th round. Use red all around 21st round.

❻ On 22nd round, join 1 piece to every 2 pieces on the previous round.

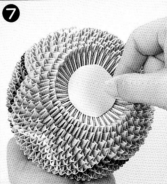

❼ Arrange overall shape, and slot in dab of glue between pieces to secure. Put bell through bottom hole, and cover it with round-cut paper.

❽ Hang decorative cord from center top, and cover the top with paper cut into a flower shape.

49

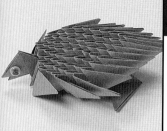

Finished size: 6"×4½"

Paper materials per turtle
80 2"×3¾" rectangles in both gold and red
(Use silver and purple for #11.)
Fold into type C triangles (see page 26).
Other materials per turtle
2 ⅜" plastic eyes

Note: For gold or silver, origami paper is used here. For red or purple, shiny craft paper is used. If using scrap paper (page 2), spray varnish over completed project to add shine and strength. Completed project may look different depending on the thickness of paper used.

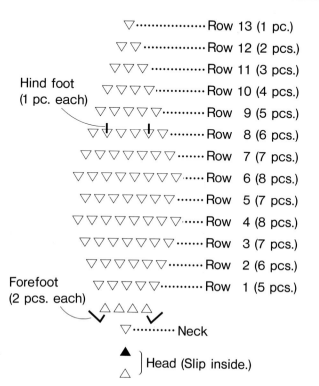

▽·················Row 13 (1 pc.)
▽ ▽················Row 12 (2 pcs.)
▽ ▽ ▽··············Row 11 (3 pcs.)
Hind foot (1 pc. each)
▽ ▽ ▽ ▽············Row 10 (4 pcs.)
▽ ▽ ▽ ▽ ▽··········Row 9 (5 pcs.)
▽ ▽ ▽ ▽ ▽ ▽········Row 8 (6 pcs.)
▽ ▽ ▽ ▽ ▽ ▽ ▽······Row 7 (7 pcs.)
▽ ▽ ▽ ▽ ▽ ▽ ▽ ▽····Row 6 (8 pcs.)
▽ ▽ ▽ ▽ ▽ ▽ ▽······Row 5 (7 pcs.)
▽ ▽ ▽ ▽ ▽ ▽ ▽ ▽····Row 4 (8 pcs.)
▽ ▽ ▽ ▽ ▽ ▽ ▽······Row 3 (7 pcs.)
▽ ▽ ▽ ▽ ▽ ▽········Row 2 (6 pcs.)
Forefoot (2 pcs. each)
▽ ▽ ▽ ▽ ▽··········Row 1 (5 pcs.)
△ △ △ △
▽··········· Neck
▲ ⎫
△ ⎭ Head (Slip inside.)

How to join hind feet

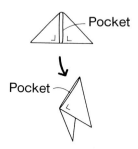

Pocket
Pocket
Unfold and insert one peak into backside.

Head assembly

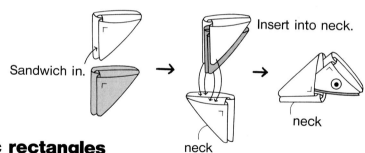

Sandwich in.   Insert into neck.
neck
neck

Laminate 2 sheets, wrong sides facing in.

How to fold basic rectangles

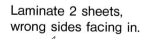

Color A (right side)

Color B (wrong side) →

Color A   Color B   Color A

Color A
Fold in diagonally on both sides. →
Color B
Color B
Fold under
Color A diagonally on both sides.

Color A
Color B

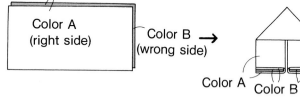

Make 1 triangles, reversing colors for ▲ (head).

▲ = Color B / Color A / Color B / Pocket

△ = Color B / Color A / Color A / Color B / Pocket

	#10	#11
A:	gold	silver
B:	red	purple

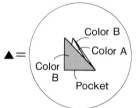

Signs for Directions

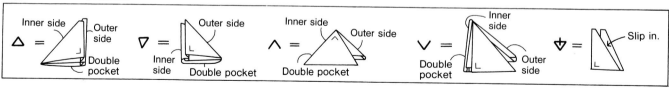

△ = Inner side / Outer side / Double pocket

▽ = Outer side / Inner side / Double pocket

∧ = Inner side / Outer side / Double pocket

∨ = Inner side / Double pocket / Outer side

⍌ = Inner side / Slip in.

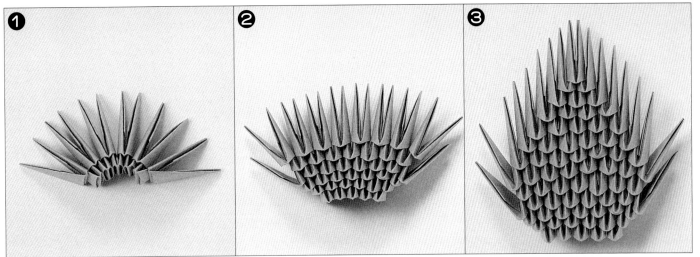

❶ Join 1st and 2nd rows referring to the diagram.

❷ Work 3rd to 6th row, increasing pieces.

❸ Work 7th to 13th row, decreasing pieces.

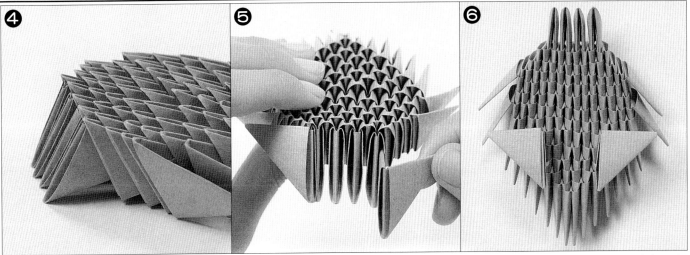

❹ Into 1st row, insert 4 pieces of neck base, reversing direction.

❺ Insert forefeet into edge pockets, in the same direction.

❻ Turn over. Insert and glue hind feet in position.

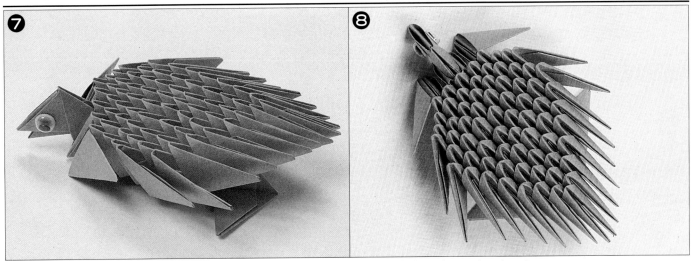

❼ Make head and insert into neck. Attach eyes.

❽ Overhead view of completed turtle.

Finished size: 8″×8″

#25, #26 Warrior's Helmet shown on page 15

Paper materials (origami cut in half)
- 159 3″×6″ rectangles in black (orange)
- 59 3″×6″ rectangles in purplish red (patterned paper)
- 59 3″×6″ rectangles in purple (patterned paper)
- 16 3″×6″ rectangles in orange (black)
- 16 1¼″×2½″ rectangles in gold
- 21 2″×3½″ rectangles in gold

Fold into type A triangles (see page 25).

Other materials
- 1 1½″ miniature family crest
   (Cut out one printed below.)
- 1 small piece of gold origami
- 1 small piece of cardboard

Tip: If using scrap paper (page 2), spray varnish over completed project to add shine and strength.

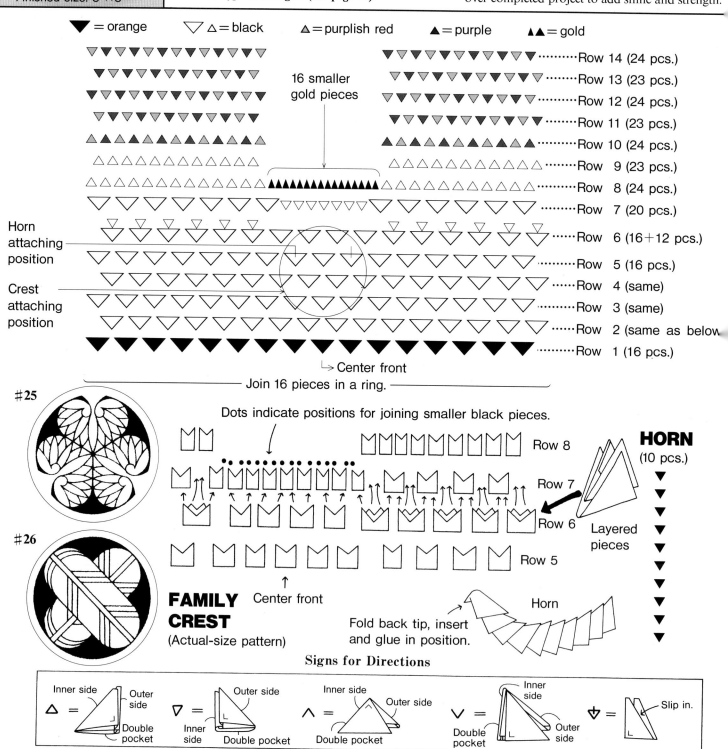

▼ = orange   ▽ △ = black   △ = purplish red   ▲ = purple   ▲▲ = gold

16 smaller gold pieces

Row 14 (24 pcs.)
Row 13 (23 pcs.)
Row 12 (24 pcs.)
Row 11 (23 pcs.)
Row 10 (24 pcs.)
Row 9 (23 pcs.)
Row 8 (24 pcs.)
Row 7 (20 pcs.)
Row 6 (16+12 pcs.)
Row 5 (16 pcs.)
Row 4 (same)
Row 3 (same)
Row 2 (same as below)
Row 1 (16 pcs.)

Horn attaching position

Crest attaching position

↳ Center front
Join 16 pieces in a ring.

#25

#26

Dots indicate positions for joining smaller black pieces.

Row 8
Row 7
Row 6
Row 5

HORN (10 pcs.)

Layered pieces

FAMILY CREST (Actual-size pattern)

↑ Center front

Horn

Fold back tip, insert and glue in position.

Signs for Directions

△ = Inner side / Outer side / Double pocket

▽ = Outer side / Inner side / Double pocket

∧ = Inner side / Outer side / Double pocket

∨ = Inner side / Double pocket / Outer side

⤓ = Slip in.

52

❶

Take 4 pieces. Apply glue to the tip of each piece and join. Make 4 of this unit.

❷

Apply glue to tips of the units and join in a ring.

❸

Work 2nd to 5th round, joining 16 pieces on each, in the same direction.

❹

For 6th round, make layered pieces: Slip 1 piece in another. Make 12 of this set-in pieces, and join in position.

❺

Completed 6th round. For the center, 4 single pieces are used according to the diagram on opposite page.

❻

On 7th round, join 13 pieces to the set-in pieces of previous round.

❼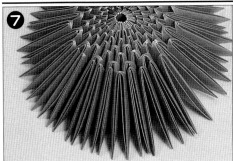

Join 7 pieces to the single pieces at the front.

❽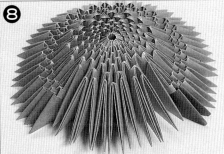

For 8th to 10th rounds, join pieces in reversed direction, leaving the front side unworked.

❾

For 9th to 14th rounds, reverse the direction again.

❿

Join 16 smaller pieces of gold to the front. Check the balance and glue.

⓫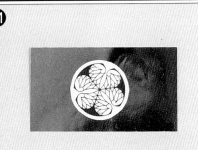

Make crest: Glue gold paper over cardboard. Layer family crest and glue. Cut $\frac{1}{8}''$ larger than the crest. (A glue gun is recommended to paste gold paper.)

⓬

Make 2 horns. Join and shape 10 pieces each as shown on opposite page. Glue on horns and crest for completed helmet.

#24 Beckoning Cat shown on page 15

Paper materials (stiff craft paper)
368 2″×3½″ rectangles in white
2 2″×4¼″ rectangles in white for ears
Fold into type C triangles (see page 26).
1 1⅛″ origami in red
Other materials
2 ½″ plastic eyes

1 ⅜″ black button for nose
22″ #28 white wrapped wire for whiskers
4″ red pipe cleaner
4″ ⅜″ red ribbon
1 miniature Japanese bell
1 pearl-head marking pin
Cardboard and gold paper for paw and gold coin

Finished size: 6″×4″

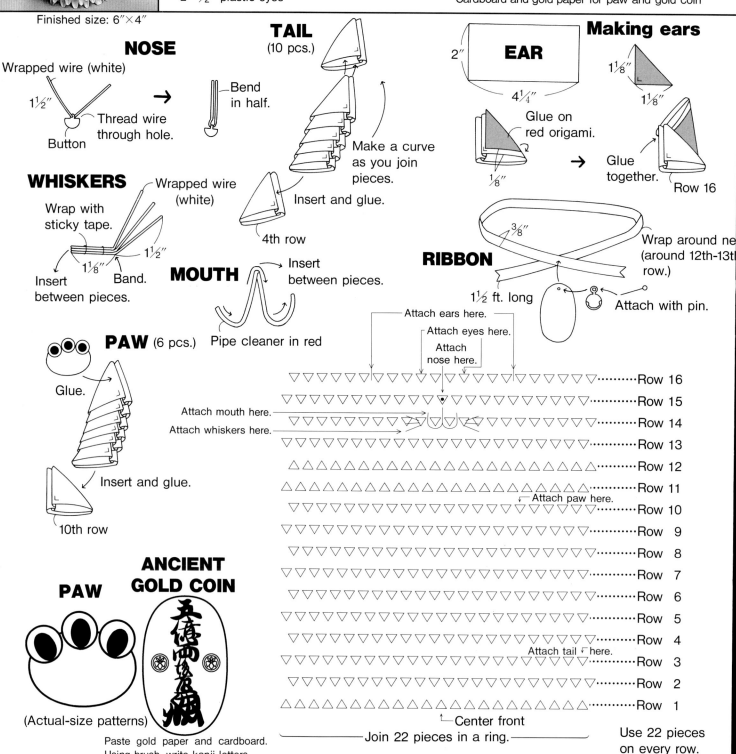

NOSE
Wrapped wire (white)
1½″
→
Thread wire through hole.
Button

TAIL
(10 pcs.)
Bend in half.
Make a curve as you join pieces.
Insert and glue.
4th row

Making ears
EAR
2″
4¼″
1⅛″
1⅛″
Glue on red origami.
⅛″
→ Glue together.
Row 16

WHISKERS
Wrap with sticky tape.
Wrapped wire (white)
1½″
1⅛″
Band.
Insert between pieces.

MOUTH
Insert between pieces.
Pipe cleaner in red

RIBBON
1½ ft. long
⅜″
Wrap around ne (around 12th-13th row.)
Attach with pin.

PAW (6 pcs.)
Glue.
Insert and glue.
10th row

PAW
ANCIENT GOLD COIN
(Actual-size patterns)
Paste gold paper and cardboard. Using brush, write kanji letters.

Attach ears here.
Attach eyes here.
Attach nose here.
Attach mouth here.
Attach whiskers here.
Attach paw here.
Attach tail here.

Row 16
Row 15
Row 14
Row 13
Row 12
Row 11
Row 10
Row 9
Row 8
Row 7
Row 6
Row 5
Row 4
Row 3
Row 2
Row 1

Center front
Join 22 pieces in a ring.
Use 22 pieces on every row.

54

① Take 5 to 6 pieces. Apply glue to tip of each piece and join together. Make more of this unit until 22 pieces are used.

② Apply glue to tips of the units and join in a ring

③ Join pieces of 2nd row.

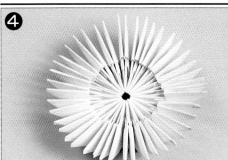

④ Completed 2nd row.

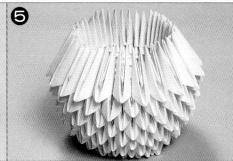

⑤ Work with 22 pieces through 3rd to 10th round, shaping as shown.

⑥ On 11th and 12th rounds, reverse direction of the joining pieces.

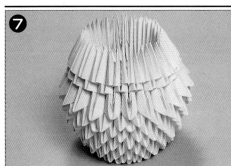

⑦ Completed 12th round.

⑧ Reverse direction of the pieces again and work 13th to 16th round.

⑨ Body is completed.

⑩ Make tail and attach to the body.

⑪ Attach ears, eyes, nose and whiskers.

⑫ Attach beckoning paw. Wind ribbon around neck, and attach gold coin and bell.

Note: Completed project may look different depending on the thickness of paper used.

Paper materials (all 2″ × 3½″ craft paper)

- 69 rectangles in white
- 157 rectangles in brown
- 157 rectangles in yellow
- 154 rectangles in black
- 1 rectangle in red

Fold into type C triangles (see page 26).

Other materials

- 2 ½″ plastic eyes
- 1 ⅜″ black button for nose
- 12″ #28 wrapped wire for whiskers
- 8″ ⅜″ ribbon in red
- 1 tiny bead wheel for center of bow
- 1 pearl-head marking pin

Finished size: 6½″ × 4½″

● **See page 55 for step-by-step instructions.**

△ △ ·················· Row 20 (2 pcs.)

Attach nose and whiskers here. △△ **Attach eyes here.** △△ ·················· Row 19 (4 pcs.)

△△△ △△△ ·················· Row 18 (6 pcs.)

△△△▲ ▲△△△ ·················· Row 17 (8 pcs.)

▽▽▼▽▼▽▼▽·▽·▽▼·▽·▼▽▼▽▼▽▼ Row 16 (22 pcs.)

▼▼▼▼▼▼▼▼▼▼▽▼·▼▼▼▼▼▼▼▼ Row 15 (same)

▽← Attach mouth here.

▽▽▽▽▽▽▽▽▽▽▽▽▽▽▽▽▽▽▽▽ Row 14 (same)

▼▼▼▼▼▼▽▽▽▽▽▽▽▼▼▼▼▼▼▼ Row 13 (same)

△△△△△△△△△△△△△△△△△△△△ Row 12 (same)

▽▽▽▽▽▽▽▽▽▽▽▽▽▽▽▽▽▽▽▽ Row 11 (same)

▼▼▼▼▼▼▽▽▽▽▽▽▽▼▼▼▼▼▼▼ Row 10 (same)

▼▼▼▼▼▽▽▽▽▽▽▽▽▽▼▼▼▼▼▼ Row 9 (same)

▽▽▽▽▽▽▽▽▽▽▽▽▽▽▽▽▽▽▽▽ Row 8 (same)

▽▽▽▽▽▽▽▽▽▽▽▽▽▽▽▽▽▽▽▽ Row 7 (same)

▼▼▼▼▼▽▽▽▽▽▽▽▽▽▼▼▼▼▼▼ Row 6 (same)

Attach tail here. ▽
▼▼▼▼▽▽▽▽▽▽▽▽▽▽▽▼▼▼▼▼ Row 5 (same)

▽▽▽▽▽▽▽▽▽▽▽▽▽▽▽▽▽▽▽▽ Row 4 (same)

▽▽▽▽▽▽▽▽▽▽▽▽▽▽▽▽▽▽▽▽ Row 3 (same)

▼▼▼▼▼▽▽▽▼▼▼▼▼▼▼▼▼▼▼▼ Row 2 (same as below)

▲▲▲▲▲▲▲▲▲▲▲▲▲▲▲▲▲▲▲▲▲▲ Row 1 (22 pcs.)

└ Center front

Join 22 pieces in a ring.

Attach ribbon here.

△ = white
△ = brown (yellow)
▲ = black
△ = red

BOW TRIM

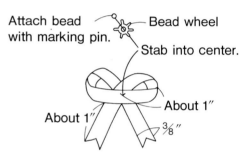

Attach bead with marking pin. — Bead wheel

Stab into center.

About 1″

About 1″

⅜″

TAIL (8 pcs.)

▲
△
▲
△
▲
△
▲
△

Row 4

Assemble into shape.

Insert and glue.

MOUTH

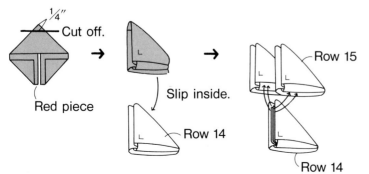

¼″
— Cut off.

Red piece

→ Slip inside.

→ Row 15

Row 14

Row 14

NOSE/WHISKERS

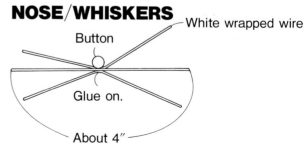

White wrapped wire

Button

Glue on.

About 4″

Note: Completed project may look different depending on the thickness of paper used.

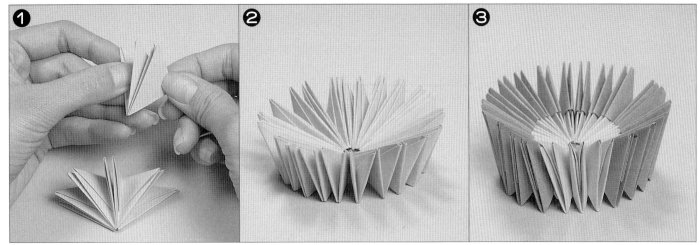

① Take 5 to 6 pieces. Apply glue to the tip of each piece and join. Repeat making this unit.

② Apply glue onto tips of each unit and join into a ring of 22 pieces.

③ Join pieces of 2nd row.

④ Work 3rd to 9th rounds referring to diagram overleaf for color.

⑤ On 10th round, reverse direction of insertion.

⑥ 10th round is completed.

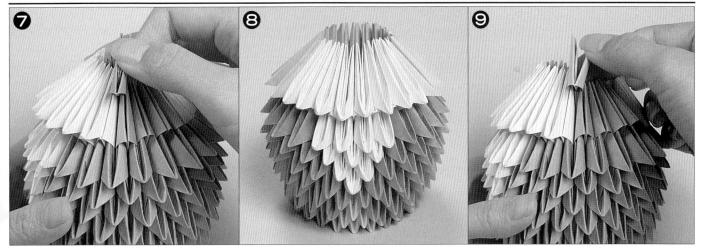

⑦ On 11th round, reverse piece direction again.

⑧ Showing 11th round completed.

⑨ Follow the diagram for color on 12th round. See overleaf for further steps.

Paper materials per each owl (all 2¼″×4½″ origami cut in half)
- 56 rectangles in white for face
- 92 rectangles in beige (gray)
- 182 rectangles in red (navy)
- 1 rectangle in red for beak

Fold into type A triangles (see page 25).

Other materials per owl
- 2 1⅛″ plastic eyes
- 1 pair glasses
- 8″ ⅛″ Japanese cord
- 1 pearl-head marking pin
- 12″ square crepe fabric in red (purple) for hat and cushion
- Cushion filler

Finished size: 5″×4½″

●See page 57 for step-by-step instructions.

Insert eyeglasses here.

△△△△△ △△△△△ ············Row 16 (10 pcs.)

△△△△△△△△△△△△ ············Row 15 (12 pcs.)

▽▽▽▽▽▽▽▽▽▽▽▽▽▽▽▽▽▽▽▽▽▽ ·········Row 14 (22 pcs.)

Attach eyes here.
▽▽▽▽▽▽▽▽▽▽▽▽▽▽▽▽▽▽▽▽▽▽ ·········Row 13 (same)

Attach mouth here.
▽▽▽▽▽▽▽▽▽▽▽▽▽▽▽▽▽▽▽▽▽▽ ·········Row 12 (same)

▽▽▽▽▽▽▽▽▽▽▽▽▽▽▽▽▽▽▽▽▽▽ ·········Row 11 (same)

△△△△△△△△△△△△△△△△△△△△△△ ·········Row 10 (same)

Attach bow here.
▼▼▼▼▼▼▼▼▼▼▽▽▽▽▼▼▼▼▼▼▼▼ ·········Row 9 (same)

▼▼▼▼▼▼▼▼▼▼▽▽▽▼▼▼▼▼▼▼▼▼ ·········Row 8 (same)

▼▼▼▼▼▼▼▼▼▼▽▽▼▼▼▼▼▼▼▼▼▼ ·········Row 7 (same)

▼▼▼▼▼▼▼▼▼▼▽▼▼▼▼▼▼▼▼▼▼▼ ·········Row 6 (same)

▼▼▼▼▼▼▼▼▼▼▼▼▼▼▼▼▼▼▼▼▼▼ ·········Row 5 (same)

▼▼▼▼▼▼▼▼▼▼▼▼▼▼▼▼▼▼▼▼▼▼ ·········Row 4 (same)

▼▼▼▼▼▼▼▼▼▼▽▽▼▼▼▼▼▼▼▼▼▼ ·········Row 3 (same)

▼▼▼▼▼▼▼▼▼▼▽▽▽▼▼▼▼▼▼▼▼▼ ·········Row 2 (same as below)

▲▲▲▲▲▲▲▲▲▲▲▲▲▲▲▲▲▲▲▲▲▲ ·········Row 1 (22 pcs.)

└Center front

└─────Join 22 pieces in a ring.─────┘

Female Male
△ = white   white
△ = beige   gray
▲ = red   navy
▽ = red   red

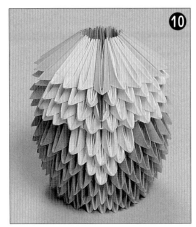

❿ Showing the front when 14 rows are done. Beak is added on 12th row.

⓫ Work 15th and 16th rows, forming ears by joining pieces in reverse direction. Attach bow, eyes and glasses for completed owl.

●Make hat and cushion with crepe fabric as illustrated on the next page.

Tip: When all pieces are joined, slot in dab of glue between pieces for a stable project.

BOW

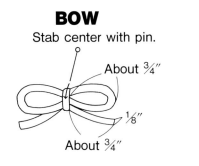

Stab center with pin.

About ¾″

⅛″

About ¾″

EYEGLASSES

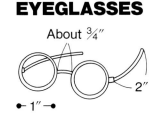

About ¾″

2″

← 1″ →

Assembly of beak

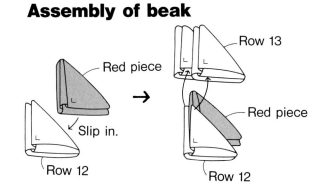

Red piece

Row 13

Slip in.

Red piece

Row 12

Row 12

CUSHION

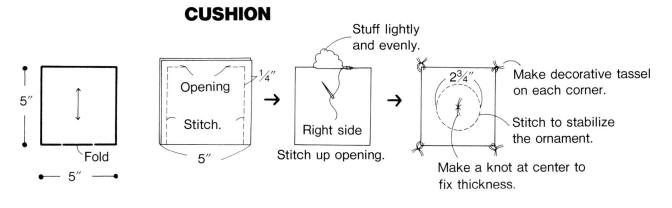

Stuff lightly and evenly.

5″

Fold

← 5″ →

Opening

Stitch.

5″

¼″

Right side

Stitch up opening.

2¾″

Make a knot at center to fix thickness.

Make decorative tassel on each corner.

Stitch to stabilize the ornament.

HAT

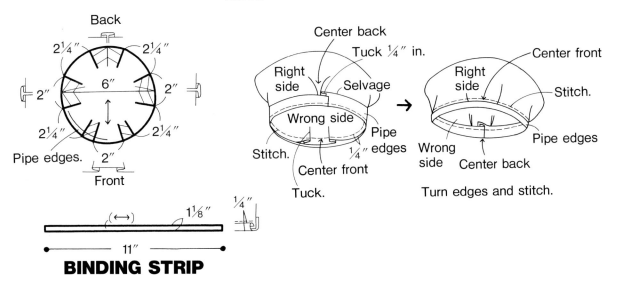

Back

2¼″   2¼″

2″   6″   2″

2¼″   2¼″

Pipe edges.   2″

Front

Center back

Tuck ¼″ in.

Right side

Selvage

Wrong side

Stitch.

Center front

Tuck.

Pipe edges

¼″

Center front

Right side

Stitch.

Pipe edges

Wrong side

Center back

Turn edges and stitch.

1⅛″   ¼″

← 11″ →

BINDING STRIP

Signs for Directions

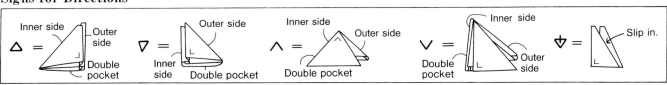

Inner side   Outer side   Double pocket

△ =

▽ =   Outer side   Inner side   Double pocket

∧ =   Inner side   Outer side   Double pocket

∨ =   Inner side   Double pocket   Outer side

⊽ =   Inner side   Slip in.

59

Paper materials (stiff craft paper)
418 2″×3½″ rectangles in yellow
55 2″×3½″ rectangles in white
Fold into type C triangles (see page 26).
Other materials
2 ½″ plastic eyes
1 ½″ pompon

Tips: When all pieces are joined, slot in dab of glue between pieces for a stable project.
Completed project may look different depending on the thickness of paper used.

Finished size: 3½″×6½″

△ = yellow
▲ = white

TAIL

▽▽▽······· Row 9 (3 pcs.)
▽▽········· Row 8 (2 pcs.)
▽▽▽······· Row 7 (3 pcs.)
▽▽▽▽····· Row 6 (4 pcs.)
▽▽▽······· Row 5 (3 pcs.)
▽▽▽▽····· Row 4 (4 pcs.)
▽▽▽······· Row 3 (3 pcs.)
▼▼········· Row 2 (2 pcs.)
▼············· Row 1 (1 pc.)

Eye attaching position

▲ ▲·············Row 22 (2 pcs.)
▲▲ ▲▲·············Row 21 (4 pcs.)
△△△ △△△·············Row 20 (6 pcs.)
△△△△ △△△△·············Row 19 (8 pcs.)
△△△△△△▽▽△△△△△△·······Row 18 (12 pcs.)
▽▽▽▽▽▽▽▽▽▽▽▽▽▽▽▽▽▽▽▽▽▽▽·Row 17 (23 pcs.)
▽▽▽▽▽▽▽▽▽▽▽▽▽▽▽▽▽▽▽▽▽▽▽··Row 16 (same)
▽▽▽▽▽▽▽▽▽▽▽▽▽▽▽▽▽▽▽▽▽▽▽·Row 15 (same)
▽▽▽▽▽▼▼▼▼▼▼▼▽▽▼▼▼▼▼▼▽▽▽▽▽··Row 14 (same)
△△△△△△△△△△▼▽▼△△△△△△△△△△△·Row 13 (same)
▽▽▽▽▽▽▽▽▽△▼▼▼△▽▽▽▽▽▽▽▽▽··Row 12 (same)
▽▽▽▽▽▽▽▽▽△▽△▽▽▽▽▽▽▽▽▽▽▽·Row 11 (same)
▽▽▽▽▽▽▽▽▽△△△▽▽▽▽▽▽▽▽▽▽▽··Row 10 (same)
▽▽▽▽▽▽▽▽▽▼▼▼▽▽▽▽▽▽▽▽▽▽▽·Row 9 (same)
▽▽▽▽▽▽▽▽▼▼▼▼▽▽▽▽▽▽▽▽▽▽▽··Row 8 (same)
▽▽▽▽▽▽▽▽▼▼▼▼▼▽▽▽▽▽▽▽▽▽▽·Row 7 (same)
▽▽▽▽▽▽▽▼▼▼▼▼▼▽▽▽▽▽▽▽▽▽▽··Row 6 (same)
▽▽▽▽▽▽▽▼▼▼▼▼▼▽▽▽▽▽▽▽▽▽▽·Row 5 (same)
▽▽▽▽▽▽▽▼▼▼▼▼▽▽▽▽▽▽▽▽▽▽··Row 4 (same)
▽▽▽▽▽▽▽▽▼▼▼▽▽▽▽▽▽▽▽▽▽▽·Row 3 (same)
▽▽▽▽▽▽▽▽▽▽▽▽▽▽▽▽▽▽▽▽▽··Row 2 (same as be
△△△△△△△△△△△△△△△△△△△△△△△ Row 1 (23 pcs.)
△△△△△△△△△△△△△△△△△△△△△△△ Reinforcement

Nose attaching position

Tail attaching position

Center front
—Join 23 pieces of 1st row in a ring.—

Tail

Insert into body and glue.

Signs for Directions

△ = Inner side / Outer side / Double pocket

▽ = Outer side / Inner side / Double pocket

∧ = Inner side / Outer side / Double pocket

∨ = Inner side / Double pocket / Outer side

⍆ = Inner side / Outer side / Slip in.

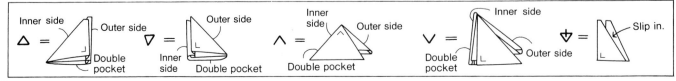

① Take 5 to 6 pieces. Apply glue to each tip and join together. Make the same unit until 23 pieces are used.

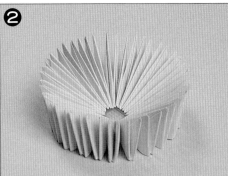

② Apply glue to tips of each unit, and join in a ring.

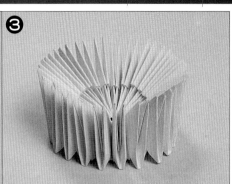

③ Join the same number pieces for the 2nd row as shown. Note the direction of pieces.

④ Turn over and join the same number pieces to reinforce.

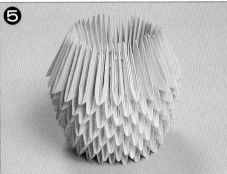

⑤ Work 3rd to 9th round, referring to the diagram for color scheme.

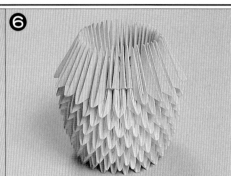

⑥ On 10th round, reverse direction of 2 center pieces.

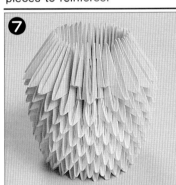

⑦ 11th round is completed. Note the direction of center pieces.

⑧ Work 12th round, still reversing the center pieces.

⑨ 13th round is completed.

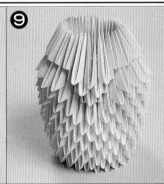

⑩ For 14th to 18th rounds, reverse all piece direction as indicated in the diagram.

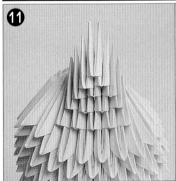

⑪ Form ears in position. Note the piecing direction.

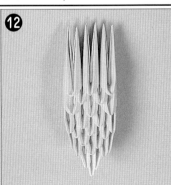

⑫ Make tail referring to the diagram.

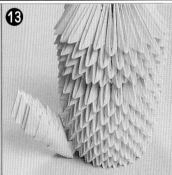

⑬ Attach tail as illustrated on the opposite page.

⑭ Attach eyes and nose for completed fox.

#27 Puppy shown on page 16

Paper materials (stiff craft paper)
314 2″×3½″ rectangles in white
54 2″×3½″ rectangles in beige
1 2″×3½″ rectangle in red
Fold into type C triangles (see page 26).

Other materials
2 ½″ black button, for eyes
Felt scrap in brown, for nose
16″ ⅜″ leather string

Finished size: 4″×6″

Tip : When all pieces are joined, slot in dab of glue between pieces for a stable project.

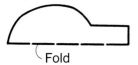 **NOSE** (Actual-size pattern)
Cut out felt and glue.

▽ =white
▼ =beige

EAR

▼ ·········· Row 6 (1 pc.)
▼ ▼ ········· Row 5 (2 pcs.)
▼ ▼ ▼ ········ Row 4 (3 pcs.)
▼ ▼ ▼ ▼ ······ Row 3 (4 pcs.)
▼ ▼ ▼ ▼ ▼ ····· Row 2 (5 pcs.)
▲ ▲ ▲ ▲ ······ Row 1 (4 pcs.)

MOUTH (Actual-size pattern)
Clip red paper, and insert into head.

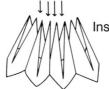

Fold

Attaching ear

↓↓↓↓

Insert each peak into head.

EAR

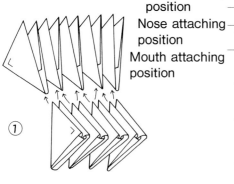

①

↓

② Insert 2 peaks only at sides.

Ear attaching position

▽▽▽▽▽↓↓↓▽▽▽▽▽▽▽▽▽▽▽▽▽↓↓↓▽▽▽ ········Row 15

Eye attaching position
▽▽▽▽▽▽▽▽▽▽▽▽▽▽▽▽▼▼▽▽▽▽▽▽ ·········Row 14

Nose attaching position
▽▽▽▽▽▽▽▽▽▽▽▽▽▽▽▼▼▽▽▽▽▽▽ ········Row 13

▽▽▽▽▽▽▽▼▼▽▽▽▽▽▽▽▽▽▽▽▽▽ ·········Row 12

Mouth attaching position
▽▽▽▽▽▽▼▼▽▽▽▽▽▽▽▽▽▽▽▽▽▽ ········Row 11

△△△△△△△△△△△△△△△△△△△△△△ ←Neck ·· Row 10

▽▽▽▽▽▽▽▽▽▽▽▽▽▽▽▽▽▽▽▽▽▽ ········Row 9

▽▽▽▽▽▽▽▽▽▽▽▽▽▽▽▽▽▽▽▽▽▽ ········Row 8

▽▽▽▽▽▽▽▽▽▽▽▽▽▽▽▽▽▽▽▽▽▽ ········Row 7

▽▽▽▽▽▽▽▼▼▽▽▽▽▽▽▽▽▽▽▽▽▽ ········Row 6

▽▽▽▽▽▽▽▼▼▼▽▽▽▽▽▼▼▽▽▽▽▽ ········Row 5

▽▽▽▽▽▽▽▽▽▽▽▽▽▽▼▼▽▽▽▽▽▽ ········Row 4

▽▽▽▽▽▽▽▽▽▽▽▽▽▽▽▽▽▽▽▽▽▽ ········Row 3

▽▽▽▽▽▽▽▽▽▽▽▽▽▽▽▽▽▽▽▽▽▽ ········Row 2

△△△△△△△△△△△△△△△△△△△△△△ ········Row 1

Center front
Join 22 pieces in a ring.

Use 22 pieces on every row.

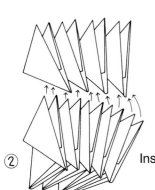

62 **Note :** Completed project may look different depending on the thickness of paper used.

1 Take 5 to 6 pieces. Apply glue to the tip of each piece and join together. Make the same unit until 22 pieces are used.

2 Apply glue to tips of each unit, and join in a ring.

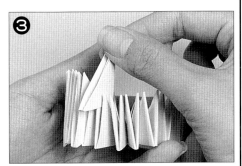

3 Work 2nd round using the same number pieces.

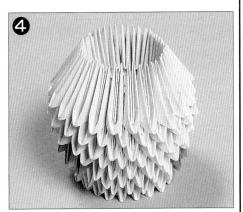

4 Work 3rd to 9th round, referring to diagram for color.

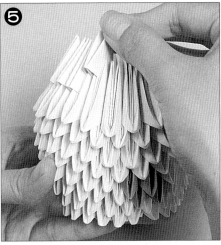

5 On 10th round, reverse piece direction.

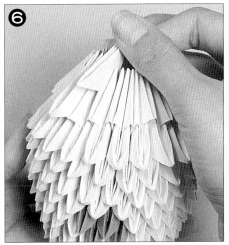

6 On 11th round, reverse direction again to the original way.

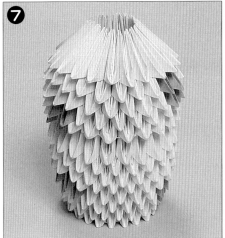

7 Completed body, consisting of 15 rounds.

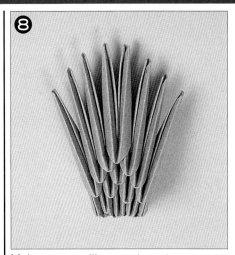

8 Make ears as illustrated on the opposite page.

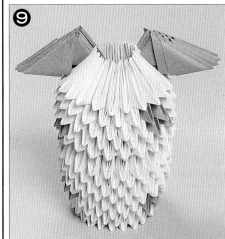

9 Attach ears by inserting into top pieces of body.

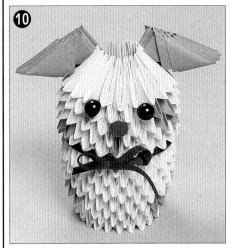

10 Attach eyes and mouth. Tie a bow with leather string for completed puppy.

Finished size: 4"×6"

#28 Panda Bear shown on page 16

Paper materials (stiff craft paper)
- 378 2"×3½" rectangles in white
- 126 2"×3½" rectangles in black
- 6 2"×3½" rectangles in black for limbs

Fold into type C triangles (see page 26).

Other materials
- 2 ¾" plastic eyes
- 1 ½" black button for nose

Note: Completed project may look different depending on the thickness of paper used.

● **See Steps 1–2 on page 61 (FOX) for the basic row.**

① Turn over and insert 24 pieces to reinforce the base.

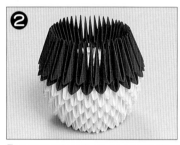

② Turn over again and work from 2nd to 11th row, referring to the diagram for color.

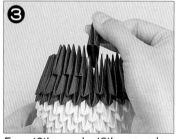

③ For 12th and 13th rounds, reverse the piece direction.

△ = white
▲ = black

Attach ears here.

Attach eyes here.

Attach nose here.

Attach fore feet here.

Neck

Attach hind feet here.

Row 20
Row 19
Row 18
Row 17
Row 16
Row 15
Row 14
Row 13
Row 12
Row 11
Row 10
Row 9
Row 8
Row 7
Row 6
Row 5
Row 4
Row 3
Row 2
Row 1

Reinforcement

Center front

Join 24 pieces of 1st row in a ring.

Use 24 pieces on every row.

● **See page 84 for actual-size patterns of ears and limb.**

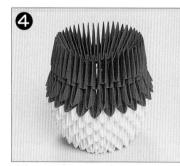

④ 13th round is completed.

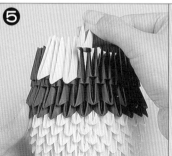

⑤ Return the piecing direction on 14th round.

⑥ Work until 20th round is done, shifting colors.

⑦ Attach eyes, nose, ears and limbs for completed panda bear.

#30 Raccoon Dog shown on page 17

Paper materials (stiff craft paper)
458 2″×3½″ rectangles in beige
 41 2″×3½″ rectangles in brown
 37 2″×3½″ rectangles in white
Fold into type C triangles (see page 26).

Other materials
2 ½″ plastic eyes
1 ½″ pompon for nose
1 silk-flower leaf
Felt scrap in dark color for navel

Note: Completed project may look different depending on the thickness of paper used.

● See page 60-61 (FOX) for making tail.

Finished size: 4″×6″

Attach ears here.

TAIL

△▽ = beige
▼ = brown
▽ = white

Row 7 ▼ ▼ ▼
Row 6   ▽ ▽
Row 5   ▽ ▽ ▽

Attach eyes here.

PAW

Row 4 ▼ ▼ ▼ ▼
Row 3 ▽ ▽ ▽
Row 2 ▼ ▼ ▼
Row 1   ▽ ▽

NAVEL
(actual-size pattern)

Attach nose here.

Attach paws here.

Attach navel here.

Attach tail here.

.... Row 20
.... Row 19
.... Row 18
.... Row 17
.... Row 16
.... Row 15
.... Row 14
.... Row 13 Neck
.... Row 12
.... Row 11
.... Row 10
.... Row 9
.... Row 8
.... Row 7
.... Row 6
.... Row 5
.... Row 4
.... Row 3
.... Row 2
.... Row 1
Reinforcement

Center front
Use 24 pieces on every row.
Join 24 pieces of 1st row in a ring.

● **EAR:** Cut out a small triangle and paste onto a beige piece. Make 2 and glue onto head.

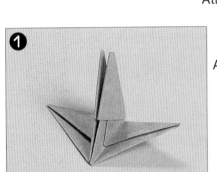

Hold 2 pieces together, pocket sides down, and insert them into pockets of another piece held in reverse direction. Make 12 of this 3-piece unit.

Join the units with 2nd row pieces to form a ring.

When the ring is formed as shown, turn over and insert pieces of reinforcement row.

Turn over again and work 3rd to 13th round, changing piece direction for neck.

Work 14th to 20th round, forming head. Attach eyes, nose, ears, navel, leaf, paws and tail for completed raccoon.

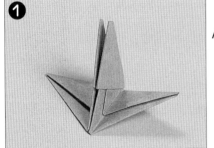

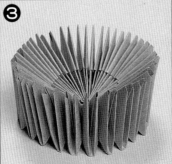

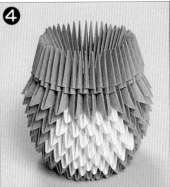

65

#33, #34 Baby Owl shown on page 19

Paper materials per owl (craft paper)
380 $1\frac{1}{2}" \times 2\frac{1}{2}"$ rectangles in light blue (light green)
79 $1\frac{1}{2}" \times 2\frac{1}{2}"$ rectangles in white
1 $1\frac{1}{2}" \times 2\frac{1}{2}"$ rectangle in red
Fold into type C triangles (see page 26).

Other materials
2 $\frac{1}{2}"$ plastic eyes
Felt scrap in gray

Note: Completed project may look different depending on the thickness of paper used.

Finished size: $4" \times 4\frac{1}{2}"$

△ = light blue (light green)
▲ = white
△ = red

Tip: When all pieces are joined, slot in dab of glue between pieces for a stable project.

Eye attaching position

△△△△   △△△△ ············Row 21 (8 pcs.)
△▲▲▲△   △▲▲▲△ ············Row 20 (10 pcs.)
△△△△△   △△△△△ ············Row 19 (10 pcs.)
▽▽▽▽▽▽▽▲▲▲▲▲ ▲▲▲▲▲▽▽▽▽▽▽▽▽·····Row 18 (24 pcs.)
▽▽▽▽▽▽▽▽▲▲▲▲ ▲▲▲▲▽▽▽▽▽▽▽▽·····Row 17 (same)
▽▽▽▽▽▽▽▽▲▲▲▲ ▲▲▲▲▽▽▽▽▽▽▽▽·····Row 16 (same)
▽▽▽▽▽▽▽▽▲▲▲▲ ▲▲▲▲▽▽▽▽▽▽▽▽·····Row 15 (same)
▽▽▽▽▽▽▽▽▼▼▼▼▼▽▼▼▼▼▼▽▽▽▽▽▽▽·····Row 14 (same)
△△△△△△△△▲▲▲▲▲▲▲△△△△△△△△·····Row 13 (same)
▽▽▽▽▽▽▽▽▼▼▼▼▼▼▽▽▽▽▽▽▽▽▽·····Row 12 (same)
▽▽▽▽▽▽▽▽▼▼▼▼▼▽▽▽▽▽▽▽▽▽·····Row 11 (same)
▽▽▽▽▽▽▽▽▼▼▼▼▽▽▽▽▽▽▽▽▽·····Row 10 (same)
▽▽▽▽▽▽▽▽▼▼▼▼▽▽▽▽▽▽▽▽·····Row 9 (same)
▽▽▽▽▽▽▽▽▼▼▼▽▽▽▽▽▽▽▽·····Row 8 (same)
▽▽▽▽▽▽▽▽▽▽▽▽▽▽▽▽▽▽·····Row 7 (same)
▽▽▽▽▽▽▽▽▽▽▽▽▽▽▽▽▽·····Row 6 (same)
▽▽▽▽▽▽▽▽▽▽▽▽▽▽▽▽·····Row 5 (same)
▽▽▽▽▽▽▽▽▽▽▽▽▽▽▽·····Row 4 (same)
▽▽▽▽▽▽▽▽▽▽▽▽▽▽·····Row 3 (same)
▽▽▽▽▽▽▽▽▽▽▽▽▽▽▽▽▽·····Row 2 (same as below)
△△△△△△△△△△△△△△△△△△△△△·······Row 1 (24 pcs.)

⌐ Center front
Join 24 pieces in a ring.

EYES

Cut out felt and glue onto head.

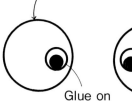

Glue on plastic eye.

EYE
(Actual-size pattern)

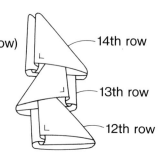
14th row
13th row
12th row

Signs for Directions

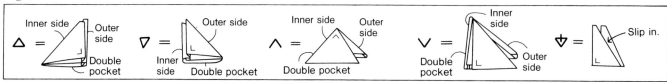

△ = Inner side / Outer side / Double pocket
▽ = Outer side / Inner side / Double pocket
∧ = Inner side / Outer side / Double pocket
∨ = Inner side / Double pocket / Outer side
⋎ = Inner side / Slip in.

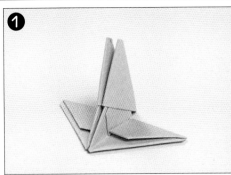

① Hold 2 pieces together, pocket sides down, and insert them into pockets of another piece held in reverse direction. Make 12 of this 3-piece unit.

② Join units with 2nd row pieces to form a ring.

③ Completed 2nd round.

④ Work 3rd to 12th round, shifting colors as indicated.

⑤ On 13th round, reverse piece direction to form neck.

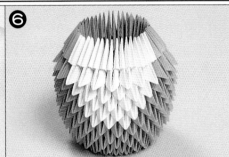

⑥ 13th round is completed.

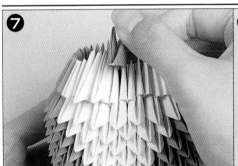

⑦ On 14th round, return the piece direction and insert a red piece for mouth in center front.

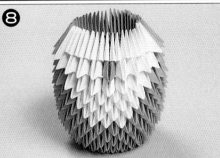

⑧ On 15th round, reverse direction of white pieces only.

⑨ Work 15th to 18th round, reversing direction of white pieces.

⑩ Make ears between 19th to 21st row.

⑪ 21st row is completed.

⑫ Attach eyes for completed baby owl.

#31 Black Owls shown on page 18

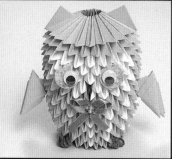

Paper materials per owl (stiff craft paper)
Parent owl:
   355   $2\frac{3}{4}''\times5''$ rectangles in black
    61   $2\frac{3}{4}''\times5''$ rectangles in pale pink
     1   $2''\times3\frac{1}{2}''$ rectangle in red
Child owl:
   355   $2''\times3\frac{1}{2}''$ rectangles in black
    61   $2''\times3\frac{1}{2}''$ rectangles in pale pink
     1   $1\frac{1}{2}''\times2\frac{3}{4}''$ rectangle in red
Fold into type C triangles (see page 26).

Other materials per owl
  $11''$ thick pipe cleaner in brown, for feet
  2 $1\frac{1}{8}''$ plastic eyes
  Felt scrap in brown
  $10''$ $\frac{3}{8}''$ ribbon in red
  1 bead wheel
  1 pearl-head marking pin

◆Instructions are the same for both parent and child owl. Paper size is the only difference.

Finished size: Parent: $4\frac{1}{2}''\times6''$
            Child: $3\frac{1}{2}''\times5''$

Tip: When all pieces are joined, slot in dab of glue between pieces for a stable project.

Attach ears here.

△ = black
▲ = pale pink
∨ = red

········ Row 17
······· Row 16
······· Row 15

Attach eyes here. → ······· Row 14
······· Row 13

Attach mouth here. → ······· Row 12
······· Row 11

Attach bow here.
Attach wings here. → ······ Row 10
······ Row 9
······ Row 8
······ Row 7
······ Row 6
······ Row 5
······ Row 4
······ Row 3
······ Row 2
Attach feet here. → + ———— + ······ Row 1

Reinforcement
⌐Center front
Join 22 pieces of 1st row in a ring.

Use 22 pieces on every row.

WING

∇ ······· Row 5
∇ ∇ ······ Row 4
∇ ∇ ∇ ····· Row 3
∇ ∇ ∇ ∇ ···· Row 2
△ ········ Row 1

BOW

Stab marking pin through bead. — Bead wheel

About $1\frac{1}{8}''$ About $1\frac{1}{8}''$

(Use thinner ribbon for child owl.)

EYE

(Actual-size pattern)

Parent

Child

(felt)

Making feet

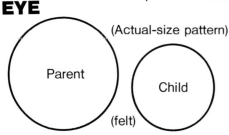

Wind pipe cleaner around a round stick such as a pencil. → Cut in half and push in ends. → Arrange shape and glue onto bottom of body.

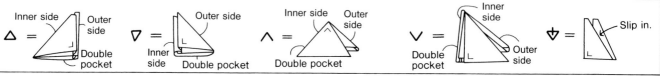

△ = Inner side / Outer side / Double pocket

▽ = Outer side / Inner side / Double pocket

∧ = Inner side / Outer side / Double pocket

∨ = Inner side / Double pocket / Outer side

⇓ = Slip in.

①

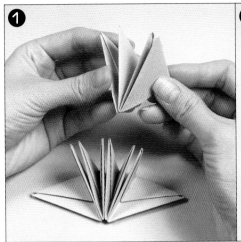

Take 5 pieces. Apply glue to the tip of each piece and join. Make the same unit until 22 pieces are used.

②

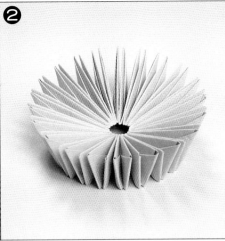

Apply glue onto tips of each unit, and join in a ring to form 1st row.

③

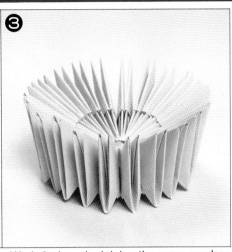

Work 2nd row by joining the same number of pieces as shown.

④

Work the reinforcing row. Turn over and insert the same number of pieces securely. Turn over again.

⑤

Work until 10th round is done, changing colors as shown in the diagram.

⑥

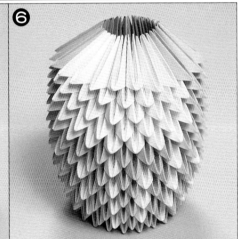

Work 11th to 15th round according to the diagram.

⑦

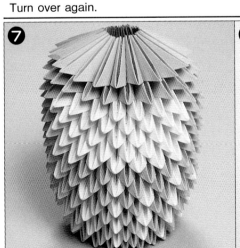

Complete body with 16th and 17th rounds.

⑧

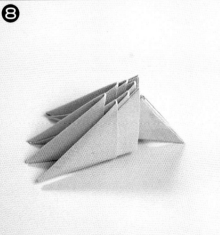

Make wings according to the diagram.

⑨

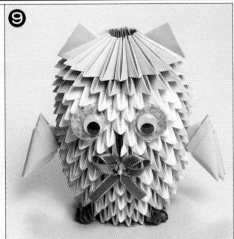

Cut out felt for eyes, and glue plastic eyes on. Insert mouth triangle in position. Glue on ears, eyes, bow and feet for completed owl. 69

♯32 Blue Owls shown on page 18

Paper materials (craft paper)
Parent owl:
  355 $2\frac{3}{4}$"×5" rectangles in blue
   61 $2\frac{3}{4}$"×5" rectangles in ivory
    1 2"×$3\frac{1}{2}$" rectangle in red
Child owl:
  355 2"×$3\frac{1}{2}$" rectangles in blue
   61 2"×$3\frac{1}{2}$" rectangles in ivory
    1 $1\frac{1}{4}$"×$2\frac{3}{4}$" rectangle in red
Fold into type C triangles (see page 26).

Other materials
  10" thick(thin) pipe cleaner in brown (lime green)
  2 1" ($\frac{3}{4}$") plastic eyes
  12" $\frac{3}{8}$"($\frac{1}{8}$") ribbon
  1 each wheel bead and pearl-head marking pin

Tips: When all pieces are joined, slot in dab of glue between pieces for a stable project. Completed project may look different depending on the thickness of paper used.

Finished size: Parent: $4\frac{1}{2}$"×6"
          Child: $3\frac{1}{2}$"×5"

Attach ears here.↓

Use 22 pieces on every row.

▽▽▽▽▽▽▽|▽▽▽▽▽▽▽▽▽▽|▽▽▽▽▽ ······Row 17
▽▽▽▽▽▽▽▽▽▽▽▽▽▽▽▽▽▽▽▽▽▽ ········Row 16
▽▽▽▽▽▽▽▼▼▼▼▼▼▼▽▽▽▽▽▽▽▽ ······Row 15

Attach eyes here. ▽▽▽▽▽▽▼▼·▼▼·▼▼▽▽▽▽▽▽▽ ······Row 14
Attach mouth here. ▽▽▽▽▽▼▼▼▼▼▼▼▼▽▽▽▽▽▽▽ ······Row 13
▽▽▽▽▽▽▼▼▼▼▼▼▽▽▽▽▽▽▽▽ ········Row 12
▽▽▽▽▽▽▽▼▼▼▽▽▼▼▼▽▽▽▽▽▽▽ ······Row 11

Attach wings here. → ▽▽▽▽▽▽▽▽▽▽▽▽▽▽▽▽▽▽▽▽▽ ········Row 10
▽▽▽▽▽▽▼↓▽▽▽▽▽↓▽▽▽▽▽▽▽ ······Row 9
▽▽▽▽▽▽▽▽▽▼▼·▼▽▽▽▽▽▽▽▽▽ ······Row 8

Attach ribbon here. ▽▽▽▽▽▽▽▽▽▼▽▽▽▽▽▽▽▽▽▽▽ ······Row 7
▽▽▽▽▽▽▽▽▽▼▼▼▽▽▽▽▽▽▽▽ ········Row 6
▽▽▽▽▽▽▽▽▽▽▼▽▼▽▽▽▽▽▽▽▽▽ ······Row 5
▽▽▽▽▽▽▽▽▽▼▽▼▽▼▽▼▽▽▽▽▽ ········Row 4
▽▽▽▽▽▽▽▽▼▽▼▽▽▼▽▼▽▽▽▽▽ ······Row 3
▽▽▽▽▽▽▽▼▽▼▽▽▼▽▼▽▽▽▽▽ ········Row 2

Attach feet here.→ + △ △ △ △ △ △ △ △ + △ △ △ △ △ △ △ △ △ Row 1
△△△△△△△△△△△△△△△△△△△△△△ Reinforcement
               ↳→ Center front
——— Join 22 pieces of 1st row in a ring. ———

WING
Row 5 ···· ▽
Row 4 ··· ▽ ▽
Row 3 ··· ▽ ▽
Row 2 · ▽ ▽ ▽
Row 1 ···· △

△ = blue
▲ = ivory
∨ = red

BOW
Stab marking pin through bead.
Bead wheel

About $1\frac{1}{2}$"(1")
About $1\frac{1}{2}$"(1")

(Use thinner ribbon for child owl.)

●**See previous page for step-by-step instructions.**

Making feet

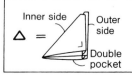

Wind pipe cleaner around a round stick such as a pencil.

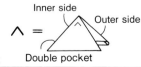

Cut in half and push in ends.

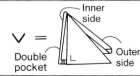

Arrange shape and glue onto bottom of body.

Signs for Directions

Inner side / Outer side / Double pocket	Inner side / Outer side / Double pocket	Inner side / Outer side / Double pocket	Inner side / Outer side / Double pocket	Slip in.
△ =	▽ =	∧ =	∨ =	⩔ =

①

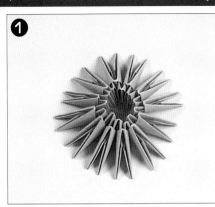

Insert adjoining points of 1st row into a 2nd row piece in the same direction. Add another piece and repeat until 12 pieces are joined on each round.

②

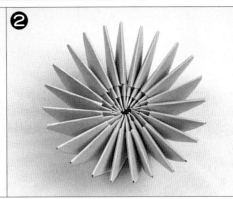

Turn over.

③

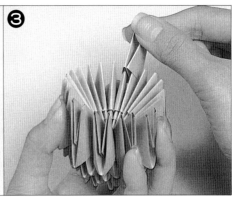

Holding it in one hand, work 3rd round, gluing each piece.

④

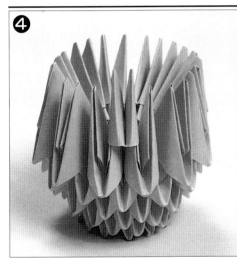

Work in the same manner until 6th round is done. Reverse direction of center pieces on 7th and remaining rounds, referring to the diagram on page 73.

⑤

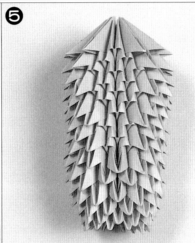

Work according to the diagram until 16 rounds are done. The bottom (chest) side is flattened.

⑥

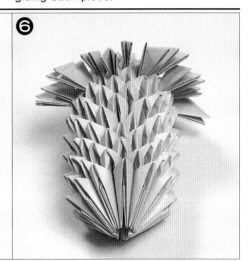

Turn around and make base of tail feather: Join 6 pieces onto 5th row from top, and 7 onto 6th row, referring to the diagram. This makes the 1st row (13 pieces). Glue each to secure.

⑦

Work 2nd row of 26 pieces, alternating colors.

⑧

Join 25 pieces of 3rd row.

⑨

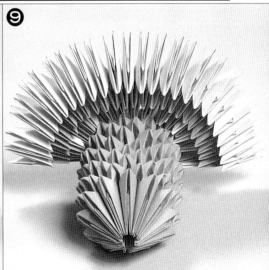

Join 26 pieces of 4th row.

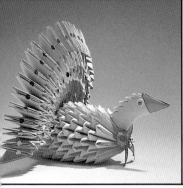

Paper materials (all 2¼"×4" craft paper)
253 rectangles in yellow
27 rectangles in lime green
39 rectangles in mint green
28 rectangles in orange
1 rectangle in red
Fold into type C triangles (see page 26).
1 each, gold and silver origami

Other materials
2 ⅜" plastic eyes
1 bead wheel
1 pearl-head marking pin

Note: Completed project may look different depending on the thickness of paper used.

Finished size: 9½"×6"

●See previous page for step-by-step instructions.

TAIL FEATHER

▽▽▽▽▽▽▽▽▽▽▽▽▽▽▽▽▽▽▽▽▽▽▽▽▽▽▽▽·Row 6 (28 pcs.) orange
▽▽▽▽▽▽▽▽▽▽▽▽▽▽▽▽▽▽▽▽▽▽▽▽▽··Row 5 (27 pcs.) mint green
▼▼▼▼▼▼▼▼▼▼▼▼▼▼▼▼▼▼▼▼▼▼▼▼····Row 4 (26 pcs.) lime green
▽▽▽▽▽▽▽▽▽▽▽▽▽▽▽▽▽▽▽▽▽▽▽······Row 3 (25 pcs.) yellow
▽▽▽▽▽▽▽▽▽▽▽▽▽▽▽▽▽▽▽▽▽▽····Row 2 (26 pcs.) lime/yellow
▽ ▽ ▽ ▽ ▽ ▽ ▽ ▽ ▽ ▽ ▽ ▽ ▽······Row 1 (13 pcs.) yellow

↖Center front
——Join 13 pieces to 5th and 6th rows of body.——

Shaping sides

(continued from page 71)

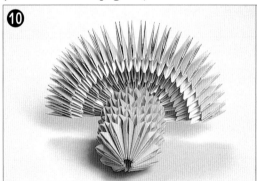

❿ Join 27 pieces of 5th row.

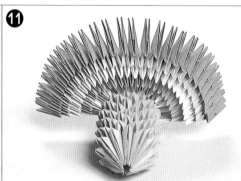

⓫ Join 28 pieces for the final row.

⓬ Make head/neck. Glue on eyes.

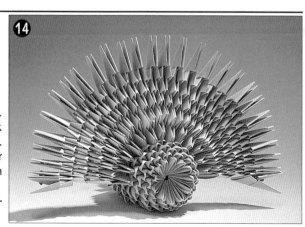

⓭ Attach neck to body. Tie ribbon around neck and pin bead wheel. Glue on gold and silver confetti or spangles on tail feather.
⓮ Rear view of completed peacock.

△ = yellow
△ = lime yellow
▲ = red (beak)
Dots: Using a puncher, cut out dots of
gold and silver origami paper. Glue
them along 4th and 6th rows.

BODY

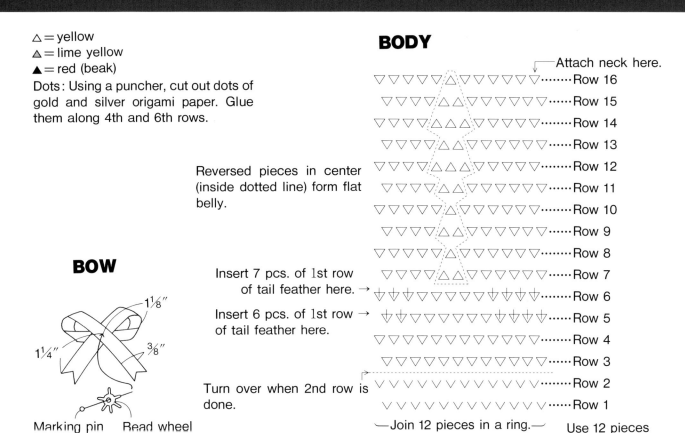

Attach neck here.

Row 16
Row 15
Row 14
Row 13
Row 12
Row 11
Row 10
Row 9
Row 8
Row 7
Row 6
Row 5
Row 4
Row 3
Row 2
Row 1

Reversed pieces in center
(inside dotted line) form flat
belly.

Insert 7 pcs. of 1st row
of tail feather here. →

Insert 6 pcs. of 1st row →
of tail feather here.

Turn over when 2nd row is
done.

— Join 12 pieces in a ring. —

Use 12 pieces
on every row.

BOW

1⅛"

1¼"

⅜"

Marking pin   Bead wheel

HEAD/NECK (11 pcs.)

Attach eyes here.

▲
△
△
△
△
△
△
△
△ Attach
bow here.
△

Make a curve.

Insert and glue.

Row 16 of body

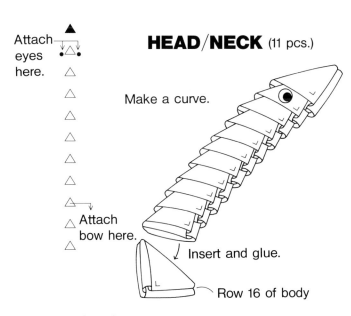

2nd row of
tail feather

1st row of tail
feather (right end)

Insert and glue.

6th row of body

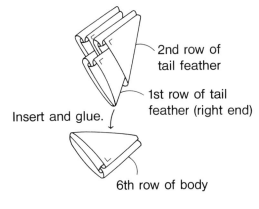

Tip: When all pieces are joined, slot in dab of
glue between pieces for a stable project.

Signs for Directions

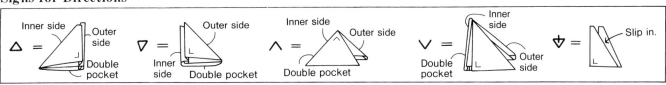

Inner side Outer side Double pocket
△ =

Inner side Outer side Double pocket
▽ =

Inner side Outer side Double pocket
∧ =

Inner side Outer side Double pocket
∨ =

Inner side Outer side Slip in.
⭣ =

#39, #40 Black Swan shown on page 20

Paper materials (all 2″×3½″ craft paper)

#39: 383 rectangles in gray
192 rectangles in black
1 rectangle in gold

#40: 470 rectangles in black
63 rectangles in gold
42 rectangles in silver

1 rectangle in red
Fold into type C triangles (see page 26).

Other materials per bird
2 ⅜″ plastic eyes
2′ ¾″ ribbon in silver

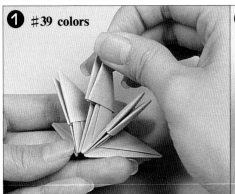

❶ #39 colors

❷

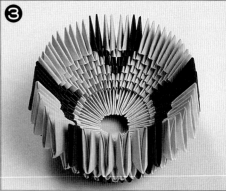

❸

Hold 2 pieces, pocket sides down, and right angles away from you. Insert 2 adjoining peaks of them into 1 piece held in reverse direction. Join 2 of this unit with 1 piece as shown.

Continue joining units until all 32 pieces are joined in a ring, for 2 rounds. This makes 1st and 2nd rounds.

Work 3rd to 7th round according to the color chart on opposite page.

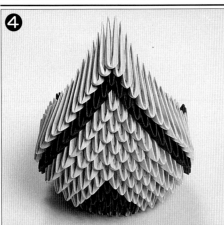

❹

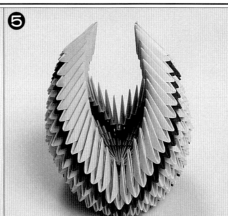

❺

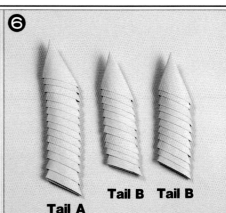

❻

Tail A Tail B Tail B

On 8th row, start forming wings separately.

Both wings are completed with 21st row.

Make 3 tail wings.

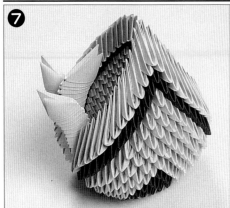

❼

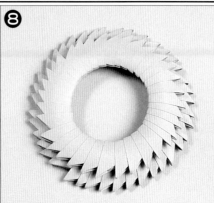

❽

❾

Join tail wings in position, curving tail A inward, tails B outward.

Make pedestal. Join 33 pieces in a ring. Make another ring with 40 pieces and glue each other.

Attach head/neck and eyes to body, and glue onto pedestal. Tie a bow around neck for completed swan.

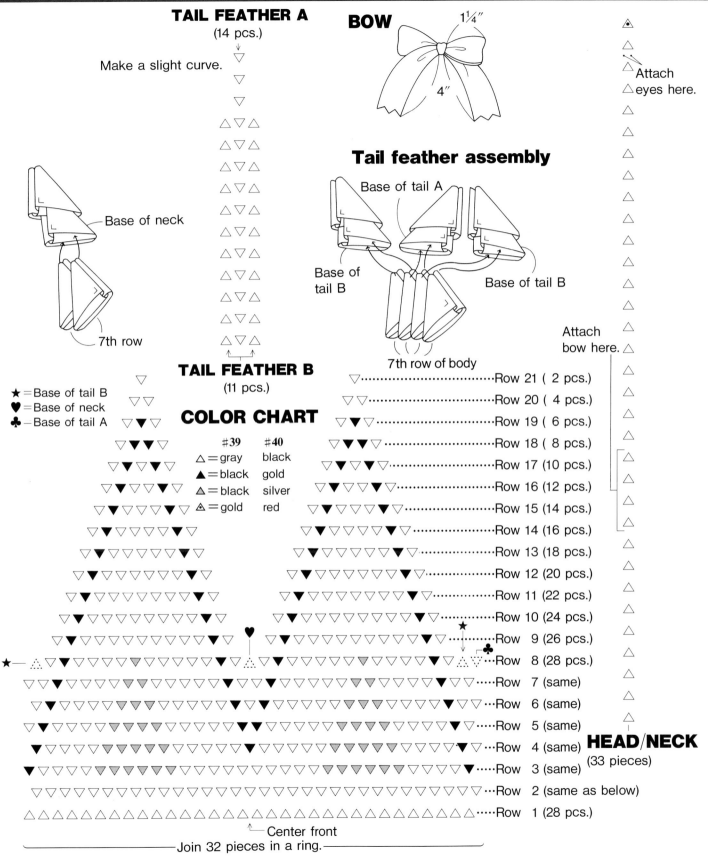

TAIL FEATHER A
(14 pcs.)

Make a slight curve.

Base of neck

7th row

TAIL FEATHER B
(11 pcs.)

★ = Base of tail B
♥ = Base of neck
♣ = Base of tail A

COLOR CHART

	#39	#40
△ =	gray	black
▲ =	black	gold
△ =	black	silver
△ =	gold	red

BOW

1¼″

4″

Attach eyes here.

Tail feather assembly

Base of tail A

Base of tail B

Base of tail B

7th row of body

Attach bow here.

Row 21 (2 pcs.)
Row 20 (4 pcs.)
Row 19 (6 pcs.)
Row 18 (8 pcs.)
Row 17 (10 pcs.)
Row 16 (12 pcs.)
Row 15 (14 pcs.)
Row 14 (16 pcs.)
Row 13 (18 pcs.)
Row 12 (20 pcs.)
Row 11 (22 pcs.)
Row 10 (24 pcs.)
Row 9 (26 pcs.)
Row 8 (28 pcs.)
Row 7 (same)
Row 6 (same)
Row 5 (same)
Row 4 (same)
Row 3 (same)
Row 2 (same as below)
Row 1 (28 pcs.)

Center front

Join 32 pieces in a ring.

HEAD/NECK
(33 pieces)

#37, #38 Rainbow Swan shown on page 20

Paper materials (all 3″ origami cut in half)
- 32 rectangles in white
- 38 rectangles in red
- 81 rectangles in orange
- 39 rectangles in deep orange
- 37 rectangles in yellow
- 4 rectangles in lemon yellow
- 70 rectangles in pink
- 41 rectangles in greenish yellow
- 40 rectangles in green
- 38 rectangles in light blue
- 8 rectangles in pale blue
- 3 rectangles in navy
- 41 rectangles in blue
- 7 rectangles in lavender
- 8 rectangles in crimson
- 39 rectangles in purple
- 35 rectangles in brown

Fold into type A triangles (see page 25).

Other materials
- 2 $\frac{1}{4}$″ plastic eyes
- 8″ $\frac{1}{4}$″ ribbon in yellow
- 1 bead wheel
- 1 pearl-head marking pin

◆For #38, place each color of body diagonally.

Finished size: $4\frac{3}{8}$″×6″

Row A: green
Row B: orange
Row C: pale blue
Row D: pink
Row E: deep orange

Row F: blue
Row G: red
Row H: navy
Row I: greenish yellow
Row J: yellow

Row K: light blue
Row L: crimson
Row M: purple
Row N: brown
Row O: lemon yellow
Row P: lavender

#37 COLOR CHART   Change color so that each color runs diagonally on wings.

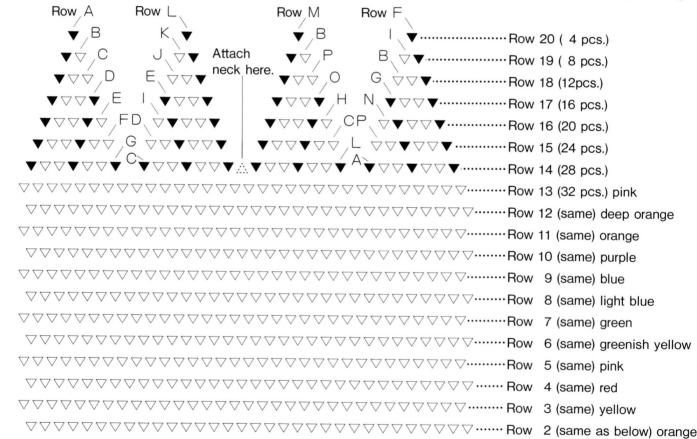

Row 20 (4 pcs.)
Row 19 (8 pcs.)
Row 18 (12pcs.)
Row 17 (16 pcs.)
Row 16 (20 pcs.)
Row 15 (24 pcs.)
Row 14 (28 pcs.)
Row 13 (32 pcs.) pink
Row 12 (same) deep orange
Row 11 (same) orange
Row 10 (same) purple
Row 9 (same) blue
Row 8 (same) light blue
Row 7 (same) green
Row 6 (same) greenish yellow
Row 5 (same) pink
Row 4 (same) red
Row 3 (same) yellow
Row 2 (same as below) orange
Row 1 (32 pcs.) brown

Attach neck here.

Center front

Join 32 pieces in a ring.

Make head/neck with 1 red and 32 white pieces.

●For step-by-step instructions, see page 74.

❶

Hold 2 pieces, pocket sides down, and right angles away from you. Insert 2 adjoining peaks of them into 1 piece held in reverse direction.

❷

Join 2 units with 1 piece as shown. Continue joining units until all 27 pieces are joined in a ring.

❸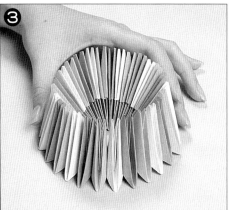

Continue joining units until all 27 pieces are joined in a ring. This makes 1st and 2nd rounds. Note the color scheme.

❹

Turn over and insert 27 pieces to reinforce the bottom.

❺

Turn over again.

❻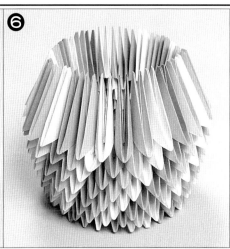

Work with colors referring to the diagram on page 78. The above shows the stage when 9th round is done.

❼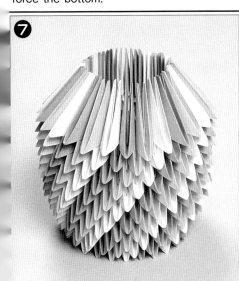

Continue until 12th round is done.

❽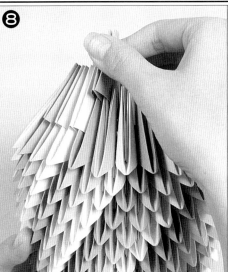

Reverse piece direction for 13th to 15th rounds.

❾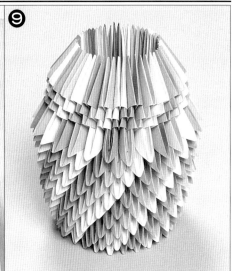

Completed vase.

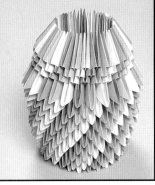

#45 Vase shown on page 22

Paper materials (all 2¼″×4¼″ craft paper)
- 153 rectangles in green
- 153 rectangles in yellow
- 126 rectangles in white

Fold into type C triangles (see page 26).

Tips: Before gluing pieces, fix shape by placing a container inside.

Note: Completed project may look different depending on the thickness of paper used.

Finished size: 6″×9″

●**See previous page for step-by-step instructions.**

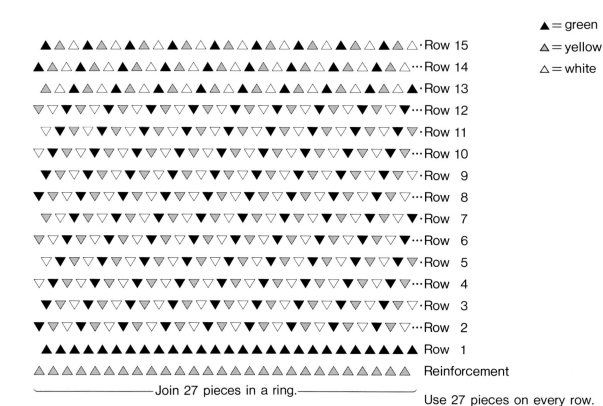

▲ = green
△ = yellow
△ = white

▲△△▲△▲△▲△▲△▲△▲△▲△▲△▲△▲△▲△·Row 15
▲△△▲△▲△▲△▲△▲△▲△▲△▲△▲△▲△△···Row 14
△△▲△▲△▲△▲△▲△▲△▲△▲△▲△▲△▲·Row 13
▽▽▼▽▼▽▼▽▼▽▼▽▼▽▼▽▼▽▼▽▼▽▼···Row 12
▽▼▽▼▽▼▽▼▽▼▽▼▽▼▽▼▽▼▽▼▽▼▽·Row 11
▽▼▽▼▽▼▽▼▽▼▽▼▽▼▽▼▽▼▽▼▽▼▽···Row 10
▼▽▽▼▽▼▽▼▽▼▽▼▽▼▽▼▽▼▽▼▽▽·Row 9
▼▽▼▽▼▽▼▽▼▽▼▽▼▽▼▽▼▽▼▽▽···Row 8
▽▽▼▽▼▽▼▽▼▽▼▽▼▽▼▽▼▽▼▽▽▼·Row 7
▽▼▽▼▽▼▽▼▽▼▽▼▽▼▽▼▽▼▽▼▼···Row 6
▽▼▽▼▽▼▽▼▽▼▽▼▽▼▽▼▽▼▽▼▼·Row 5
▽▼▽▼▽▼▽▼▽▼▽▼▽▼▽▼▽▼▽▼▼···Row 4
▼▽▼▽▼▽▼▽▼▽▼▽▼▽▼▽▼▽▼▽▽·Row 3
▼▽▽▼▽▼▽▼▽▼▽▼▽▼▽▼▽▼▽▼▽···Row 2
▲▲▲▲▲▲▲▲▲▲▲▲▲▲▲▲▲▲▲▲▲▲▲ Row 1
△△△△△△△△△△△△△△△△△△△△△△△ Reinforcement

————— Join 27 pieces in a ring.—————

Use 27 pieces on every row.

#46, #47 Basket shown on page 23

Take .5 pieces. Apply glue to the tips of each piece and join together. Make 6 of this unit.

Apply glue onto tips of each unit, and join in a ring. This makes 1st row.

Work 2nd row, reversing the piece direction.

Work in the same manner until 9th row is done.

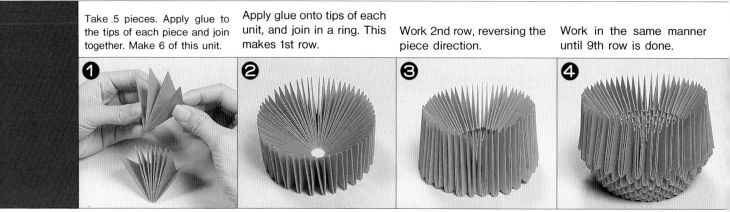

❶ ❷ ❸ ❹

#46, #47 Basket shown on page 23

Paper materials for #47 (half-cut origami)
374 3″×6″ rectangles in orange
Fold into type A triangles (see page 25).
Other materials:
10″ 1⅛″ ribbon in white

◆For #46, use scrap paper cut into type B rectangles (see page 26). Spraying varnish over finished work will give shine and strength.

Finished size: 7″×7″

△ = orange

HANDLE (7 pcs.)

Row 18 (2 pcs.)
Row 17 (4 pcs.)
Row 16 (6 pcs.)
Row 15 (8 pcs.)
Row 14 (10 pcs.)
Row 13 (12 pcs.)
Row 12 (14 pcs.)
Row 11 (16 pcs.)
Row 10 (18 pcs.)
Row 9 (30 pcs.)
Row 8 (same)
Row 7 (same)
Row 6 (same)
Row 5 (same)
Row 4 (same)
Row 3 (same)
Row 2 (same as below)
Row 1 (30 pcs.)

↳ Center front
── Join 30 pieces in a ring. ──

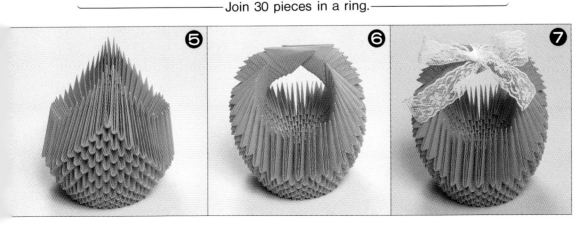

❺ On 10th to 18th rows, form bases of handle.
❻ Make a curved handle with 7 pieces and join to bases.
❼ Accentuate with a bow to conceal the joint.

79

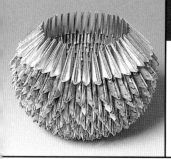

#42 Pot Cover shown on page 22

Paper materials
480 2¾″×6″ rectangles (patterned paper)
40 2¼″×4¾″ rectangles (silver *washi* paper)
Fold into type B triangles (see page 26).

Tips: Apply glue after placing flowerpot and shape accordingly.
Completed project may look different depending on the thickness of paper used.

Finished size: 9″×7″

How to form 1st row

❶ Take 5 pieces. Apply glue to the tip of each piece, and glue together. Make 6 of this unit.

❷ Apply glue onto tips of each unit, and join in a ring. This makes 1st round of 40 pieces.

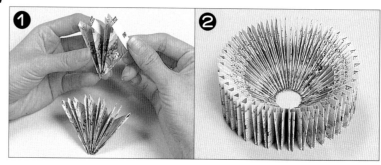

▲ = silver   △ = patterned paper

Use 40 pieces on every row.

▼▼ ······Row 13
▽▽▽▽▽▽▽▽▽▽▽▽▽▽▽▽▽▽▽▽▽▽▽▽▽▽▽▽▽▽▽▽▽▽▽▽▽▽▽ ········Row 12
▽▽▽▽▽▽▽▽▽▽▽▽▽▽▽▽▽▽▽▽▽▽▽▽▽▽▽▽▽▽▽▽▽▽▽▽▽▽▽ ·······Row 11
▽▽▽▽▽▽▽▽▽▽▽▽▽▽▽▽▽▽▽▽▽▽▽▽▽▽▽▽▽▽▽▽▽▽▽▽▽▽▽ ·······Row 10
▽▽▽▽▽▽▽▽▽▽▽▽▽▽▽▽▽▽▽▽▽▽▽▽▽▽▽▽▽▽▽▽▽▽▽▽▽▽▽ ·······Row 9
▽▽▽▽▽▽▽▽▽▽▽▽▽▽▽▽▽▽▽▽▽▽▽▽▽▽▽▽▽▽▽▽▽▽▽▽▽▽▽ ·······Row 8
▽▽▽▽▽▽▽▽▽▽▽▽▽▽▽▽▽▽▽▽▽▽▽▽▽▽▽▽▽▽▽▽▽▽▽▽▽▽▽ ·······Row 7
▽▽▽▽▽▽▽▽▽▽▽▽▽▽▽▽▽▽▽▽▽▽▽▽▽▽▽▽▽▽▽▽▽▽▽▽▽▽▽ ·······Row 6
▽▽▽▽▽▽▽▽▽▽▽▽▽▽▽▽▽▽▽▽▽▽▽▽▽▽▽▽▽▽▽▽▽▽▽▽▽▽▽ ·······Row 5
▽▽▽▽▽▽▽▽▽▽▽▽▽▽▽▽▽▽▽▽▽▽▽▽▽▽▽▽▽▽▽▽▽▽▽▽▽▽▽ ·······Row 4
▽▽▽▽▽▽▽▽▽▽▽▽▽▽▽▽▽▽▽▽▽▽▽▽▽▽▽▽▽▽▽▽▽▽▽▽▽▽▽ ·······Row 3
▽▽▽▽▽▽▽▽▽▽▽▽▽▽▽▽▽▽▽▽▽▽▽▽▽▽▽▽▽▽▽▽▽▽▽▽▽▽▽ ········Row 2
△△△△△△△△△△△△△△△△△△△△△△△△△△△△△△△△△△△△△△△ ·······Row 1

───── Join 40 pieces in a ring. ─────

#43, #44 Vase shown on page 22

Hold 2 pieces together, pocket sides down, and insert them into pockets of another piece, pocket down, facing reverse direction. Make 15 of this 3-piece unit.

Join units with 2nd row pieces.

Continue until 30 pieces are joined in a ring, at the same time forming 2nd round.

Reinforce bottom: Turn over and insert 30 pieces into pockets.

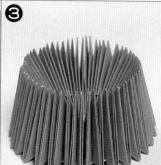

#43, #44 Vase shown on page 22

Paper materials (half-cut origami)
#43: 450   3″×6″ origami halves in green
   120   3″×6″ origami halves in yellow
Fold into type A triangles (see page 25).
#44: 570   2″×3¾″ rectangles of scrap paper
Fold into type C triangles (see page 26).

Tips: Apply glue after placing flowerpot, and shape accordingly.
Spraying varnish over finished work will give shine and strength.

▲ = yellow   △ = green

Finished size: #43: 6″×9½″
               #44: 5″×5½″

▽▽▽▽▽▽▽▽▽▽▽▽▽▽▽▽▽▽▽▽▽▽▽▽▽▽▽▽▽ ···Row 18
▼▼▼▼▼▼▼▼▼▼▼▼▼▼▼▼▼▼▼▼▼▼▼▼▼▼▼▼▼▼ ··Row 17
▽▽▽▽▽▽▽▽▽▽▽▽▽▽▽▽▽▽▽▽▽▽▽▽▽▽▽▽▽▽ ···Row 16
▼▼▼▼▼▼▼▼▼▼▼▼▼▼▼▼▼▼▼▼▼▼▼▼▼▼▼▼▼▼ ··Row 15
▽▽▽▽▽▽▽▽▽▽▽▽▽▽▽▽▽▽▽▽▽▽▽▽▽▽▽▽▽▽ ···Row 14
▽▽▽▽▽▽▽▽▽▽▽▽▽▽▽▽▽▽▽▽▽▽▽▽▽▽▽▽▽▽ ··Row 13
▽▽▽▽▽▽▽▽▽▽▽▽▽▽▽▽▽▽▽▽▽▽▽▽▽▽▽▽▽▽ ···Row 12
▽▽▽▽▽▽▽▽▽▽▽▽▽▽▽▽▽▽▽▽▽▽▽▽▽▽▽▽▽▽ ··Row 11
▼▼▼▼▼▼▼▼▼▼▼▼▼▼▼▼▼▼▼▼▼▼▼▼▼▼▼▼▼▼ ···Row 10
▽▽▽▽▽▽▽▽▽▽▽▽▽▽▽▽▽▽▽▽▽▽▽▽▽▽▽▽▽▽ ··Row 9
▽▽▽▽▽▽▽▽▽▽▽▽▽▽▽▽▽▽▽▽▽▽▽▽▽▽▽▽▽▽ ···Row 8
▼▼▼▼▼▼▼▼▼▼▼▼▼▼▼▼▼▼▼▼▼▼▼▼▼▼▼▼▼▼ ··Row 7
▽▽▽▽▽▽▽▽▽▽▽▽▽▽▽▽▽▽▽▽▽▽▽▽▽▽▽▽▽▽ ···Row 6
▽▽▽▽▽▽▽▽▽▽▽▽▽▽▽▽▽▽▽▽▽▽▽▽▽▽▽▽▽▽ ··Row 5
▽▽▽▽▽▽▽▽▽▽▽▽▽▽▽▽▽▽▽▽▽▽▽▽▽▽▽▽▽▽ ···Row 4
▽▽▽▽▽▽▽▽▽▽▽▽▽▽▽▽▽▽▽▽▽▽▽▽▽▽▽▽▽▽ ··Row 3
▽▽▽▽▽▽▽▽▽▽▽▽▽▽▽▽▽▽▽▽▽▽▽▽▽▽▽▽▽▽ ···Row 2
△△△△△△△△△△△△△△△△△△△△△△△△△△△△△ Row 1
△△△△△△△△△△△△△△△△△△△△△△△△△△△△△ Reinforcement

——— Join 30 pieces of 1st row in a ring. ———   Use 30 pieces on every row.

Turn over again and join 3rd to 6th rounds. Change color on 7th round.

❺

Work in the same manner until 11th round is done.

❻

When 18th round is done, put in a jar, shape accordingly, and slot in glue to secure.

❼

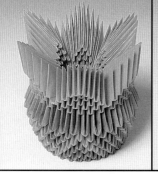

#49, #50 Star-Shaped Basket

Paper materials

#49: 300 3″×6″ origami halves in blue
      120 3″×6″ origami halves in orange
Fold into type A triangles (see page 25).
#50: 420 2″×3¾″ rectangles of scrap paper
Fold into type B triangles (see page 26).

Finished size: #49: 7″×9″   #50: 4″×4¼″

▽＝blue
▼＝orange

#49

▲ ▲ ▲ ▲ ▲ ▲·········Row 16 (6 pcs.)
▲▲ ▲▲ ▲▲ ▲▲ ▲▲ ▲▲········Row 15 (12 pcs.)
▲△▲ ▲△▲ ▲△▲ ▲△▲ ▲△▲ ▲△▲·······Row 14 (18 pcs.)
▲△△▲ ▲△△▲ ▲△△▲ ▲△△▲ ▲△△ ▲△△▲······Row 13 (24 pcs.)
▲△△△▲△△△▲△△△▲△△△▲△△△▲▲△△△▲△△△▲····Row 12 (30 pcs.)
▲△△△△▲△△△△▲△△△△▲△△△△▲△△△△▲△△△△······Row 11 (same)
△△△△△△△△△△△△△△△△△△△△△△△△△△△△△△····Row 10 (same)
▽▽▽▽▽▽▽▽▽▽▽▽▽▽▽▽▽▽▽▽▽▽▽▽▽▽▽▽▽▽······Row 9 (same)
▽▽▼▽▽▽▽▼▽▽▽▽▼▽▽▽▽▼▽▽▽▽▼▽▽▽····Row 8 (same)
▽▽▼▽▽▽▽▼▽▽▽▽▼▽▽▽▽▼▽▽▽▽▼▽▽······Row 7 (same)
▽▼▽▽▽▽▽▼▽▽▽▽▽▼▽▽▽▽▼▽▽▽▽▼▽▽▽······Row 6 (same)
▽▼▽▽▽▼▽▽▽▼▽▽▽▼▽▽▽▼▽▽▽▼······Row 5 (same)
▼▽▽▽▼▽▽▽▼▽▽▽▼▽▽▽▼▽▽▽▽▼····Row 4 (same)
▼▽▽▽▼▽▽▽▼▽▽▽▼▽▽▽▼▽▽▽▽······Row 3 (same)
▽▽▽▽▽▽▽▽▽▽▽▽▽▽▽▽▽▽▽▽▽▽▽▽▽▽▽▽▽▽····Row 2 (same as below)
△△△△△△△△△△△△△△△△△△△△△△△△△△△△△△······Row 1 (30 pcs.)

── Join 30 pieces in a ring. ──

#48 Decorative Bowl
shown on page 23

Paper materials

405 2¾″×6″ rectangles
      (patterned paper)
**Fold into type B triangles
(see page 26).**

Finished size: 7″×8″

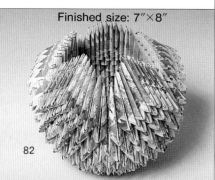

82

▽ ▽ ▽ ▽ ▽········ Row 16 (5 pcs
▽▽ ▽▽ ▽▽ ▽▽ ▽▽······ Row 15 (10 pcs
▽▽▽ ▽▽▽ ▽▽▽ ▽▽▽ ▽▽▽······ Row 14 (15 pcs
▽▽▽▽ ▽▽▽▽ ▽▽▽▽ ▽▽▽▽ ▽▽▽▽····Row 13 (20 pcs
▽▽▽▽▽ ▽▽▽▽▽ ▽▽▽▽▽ ▽▽▽▽▽ ▽▽▽▽▽··Row 12 (25 pcs
▽▽▽▽▽▽▽▽▽▽▽▽▽▽▽▽▽▽▽▽▽▽▽▽▽▽▽▽▽▽ Row 11 (30 pcs
▽▽▽▽▽▽▽▽▽▽▽▽▽▽▽▽▽▽▽▽▽▽▽▽▽▽▽▽▽▽··Row 10 (same
▽▽▽▽▽▽▽▽▽▽▽▽▽▽▽▽▽▽▽▽▽▽▽▽▽▽▽▽▽▽ Row 9 (same
▽▽▽▽▽▽▽▽▽▽▽▽▽▽▽▽▽▽▽▽▽▽▽▽▽▽▽▽▽▽··Row 8 (same
▽▽▽▽▽▽▽▽▽▽▽▽▽▽▽▽▽▽▽▽▽▽▽▽▽▽▽▽▽▽ Row 7 (same
▽▽▽▽▽▽▽▽▽▽▽▽▽▽▽▽▽▽▽▽▽▽▽▽▽▽▽▽▽▽··Row 6 (same
▽▽▽▽▽▽▽▽▽▽▽▽▽▽▽▽▽▽▽▽▽▽▽▽▽▽▽▽▽▽ Row 5 (same
▽▽▽▽▽▽▽▽▽▽▽▽▽▽▽▽▽▽▽▽▽▽▽▽▽▽▽▽▽▽··Row 4 (same
▽▽▽▽▽▽▽▽▽▽▽▽▽▽▽▽▽▽▽▽▽▽▽▽▽▽▽▽▽▽ Row 3 (same
▽▽▽▽▽▽▽▽▽▽▽▽▽▽▽▽▽▽▽▽▽▽▽▽▽▽▽▽▽▽··Row 2 (same as below)
△△△△△△△△△△△△△△△△△△△△△△△△△△△△△△ Row 1 (30 pcs

── Join 30 pieces in a ring. ──

Note: Completed project may look different depending on the thickness of paper used

1

Take 5 pieces. Apply glue to the tips of each piece and glue together. Make 6 of this unit.

2

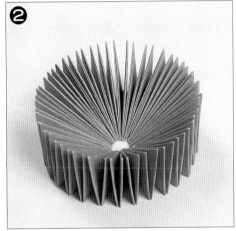

Apply glue onto tips of each unit, and join in a ring. This makes 1st round of 30 pieces.

3

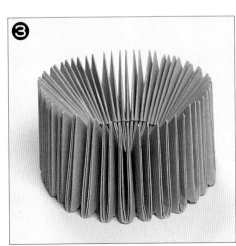

Join 2nd round, reversing the direction of the pieces.

4

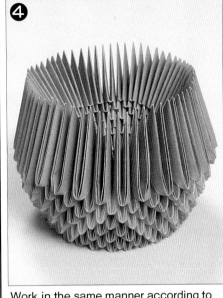

Work in the same manner according to the color chart until 9th round is done.

Tips: When all pieces are joined, slot in dab of glue between pieces for a stable project.

5

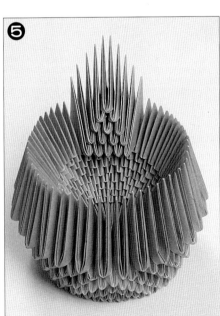

From 10th to 14th row, reverse the piece direction, and form one peak at a time, omitting the ▲ in the diagram.

6

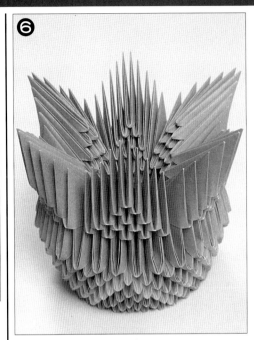

All 6 peaks are formed.

7

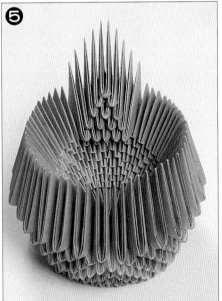

Make rim with orange color pieces, joining onto the top pieces all around, as shown in the diagram.

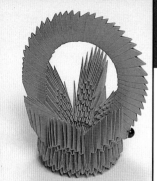

#53 Flower-Shaped Basket shown on page 24

Paper materials
305 2″×3½″ rectangles of white paper
Fold into type C triangles (see page 26).
Other materials
2 ½″ buttons

Tips: When all pieces are joined, slot in dab of glue between pieces for a stable project. Completed project may look different depending on the thickness of paper used.

Finished size: 9″×10½″

HANDLE

△＝white

△·Row 13 (1 pc.)
△·Row 12 (2 pcs.)
△···Row 11 (5 pcs.)
△△·Row 10 (8 pcs.)
△···Row 9 (9 pcs.)
△△·Row 8 (18 pcs.)
△···Row 7 (18 pcs.)
△△·Row 6 (24 pcs.)
△···Row 5 (30 pcs.)
▽·Row 4 (same)
▽···Row 3 (same)
▽·Row 2 (same as below)
Row 1 (30 pcs.)
Reinforcement

Button/handle attaching position

(40 pcs.)

↑—Center front
———Join 30 pieces in a ring.———

ACTUAL-SIZE PATTERNS FOR PANDA BEAR (page 64)

LIMB

EAR

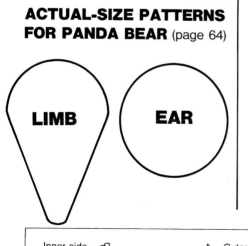

Glue button.

Handle

Insert points of basket pieces into handle.

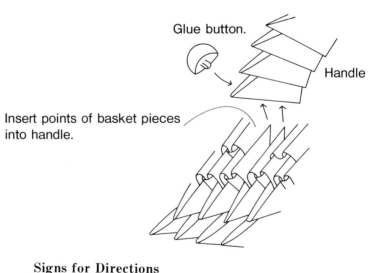

Signs for Directions

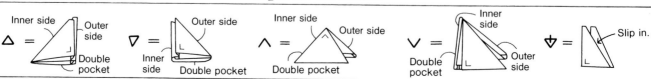

△ ＝ Inner side / Outer side / Double pocket

▽ ＝ Outer side / Inner side / Double pocket

∧ ＝ Inner side / Outer side / Double pocket

∨ ＝ Inner side / Double pocket / Outer side

⍌ ＝ Inner side / Slip in. / L

❶

Join 2 pieces by stacking a new piece onto adjacent points: Holding pocket sides down, join the new piece reversing the direction. Make 15 of this 3-piece unit.

❷

Join all units in the same manner. This forms 1st and 2nd rows.

❸

This is what it looks like after 2 rounds are done.

❹

Turn over and reinforce the bottom by inserting 30 pieces.

❺

Turn over again. Work 3rd and 4th rounds. From 5th round, change the direction of pieces.

❻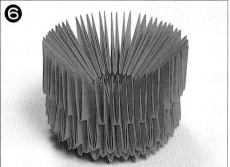

This is what it looks like after 5th round is done.

❼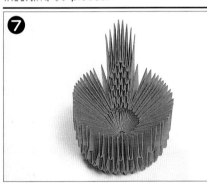

Form the tallest petal by working 6th to 13th rows.

❽

Form middle petals by working 6th to 11th rows.

❾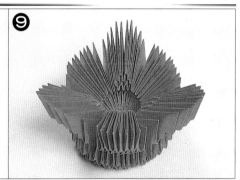

Form short petals by working 6th to 8th rows.

❿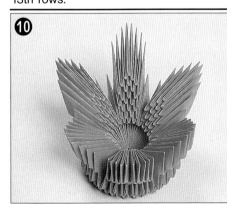

Note that petals vary.

⓫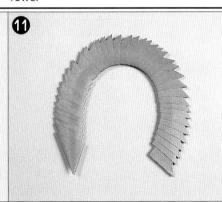

Make handle by joining 40 pieces.

⓬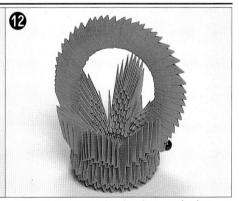

Joint handle to the basket and glue on buttons for completed basket.

#52 Basket with Handle shown on page 24

Paper materials
494 2″×3½″ rectangles of greenish yellow paper
Make type C triangles (see page 26).
Other materials
2 ¾″ buttons

Note: Completed project may look different depending on the thickness of paper used.

Finished size: 7½″×12″

●**See page 88 for step-by-step instructions.**

△=lime yellow

Use 38 pieces on every round.

⌐ Handle/Button attaching position

△△△△△△△△△△△△△△△△△△△△△△△△△△△△△△△△△△△△△△△·Row 10
▽▽▽▽▽▽▽▽▽▽▽▽▽▽▽▽▽▽▽▽▽▽▽▽▽▽▽▽▽▽▽▽▽▽▽▽▽▽···Row 9
▽▽▽▽▽▽▽▽▽▽▽▽▽▽▽▽▽▽▽▽▽▽▽▽▽▽▽▽▽▽▽▽▽▽▽▽▽▽·Row 8
▽▽▽▽▽▽▽▽▽▽▽▽▽▽▽▽▽▽▽▽▽▽▽▽▽▽▽▽▽▽▽▽▽▽▽▽▽▽···Row 7
▽▽▽▽▽▽▽▽▽▽▽▽▽▽▽▽▽▽▽▽▽▽▽▽▽▽▽▽▽▽▽▽▽▽▽▽▽▽·Row 6
▽▽▽▽▽▽▽▽▽▽▽▽▽▽▽▽▽▽▽▽▽▽▽▽▽▽▽▽▽▽▽▽▽▽▽▽▽▽···Row 5
▽▽▽▽▽▽▽▽▽▽▽▽▽▽▽▽▽▽▽▽▽▽▽▽▽▽▽▽▽▽▽▽▽▽▽▽▽▽·Row 4
▽▽▽▽▽▽▽▽▽▽▽▽▽▽▽▽▽▽▽▽▽▽▽▽▽▽▽▽▽▽▽▽▽▽▽▽▽▽···Row 3
▽▽▽▽▽▽▽▽▽▽▽▽▽▽▽▽▽▽▽▽▽▽▽▽▽▽▽▽▽▽▽▽▽▽▽▽▽▽·Row 2
△△△△△△△△△△△△△△△△△△△△△△△△△△△△△△△△△△△△△△△ Row 1
△△△△△△△△△△△△△△△△△△△△△△△△△△△△△△△△△△△△△△△ Reinforcement

⌐ Center front
Join 38 pieces of 1st row in a ring.

◁ ◁ ◁ ◁ ◁ ◁ ◁ ◁ ◁ ◁ ◁ ◁ ◁ ◁ ·············· ◁ ◁ ◁ ◁ ◁ ◁ ◁ ◁ ◁ ◁ ◁ ◁ ◁ ◁ ◁ ◁

HANDLE   Join 38 pieces and bend into U-letter shape.

◁ ◁ ◁ ◁ ◁ ◁ ◁ ◁ ◁ ◁ ◁ ◁ ◁ ◁ ·············· ◁ ◁ ◁ ◁ ◁ ◁ ◁ ◁ ◁ ◁ ◁ ◁ ◁ ◁ ◁ ◁

PEDESTAL   Join 32 pieces in a ring.

#51 Vase with Rim shown on page 24

Holding 2 pieces, pockets sides down, insert their tips into a new piece held in reverse direction.

Make the same 3-piece unit until 35 pieces are used. Join units as shown.

All units are joined, forming 1st and 2nd rounds.

Turn over and reinforce the bottom by inserting 35 pieces.

❶

❷

❸
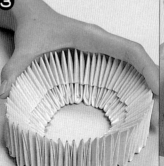

❹
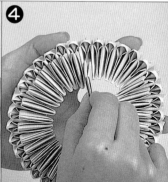

#51 Vase with Rim shown on page 24

Paper materials (all 2″×3½″ craft paper)

425	rectangles in pink
48	rectangles in blue
48	rectangles in greenish yellow
24	rectangles in yellow
24	rectangles in red
24	rectangles in black

Fold into type C triangles (see page 26).

Finished size: 7″×10″

▲ = black	△ = greenish yellow
△ = pink	▲ = red
◬ = blue	◬ = yellow

Use 35 pieces on every row.

△△△△△△△△△△△△△△△△△△△△△△△△△△△△△△△△△△△△ ····Row 15
▽▽▽▼▼▽▽▽▽▽▽▽▽▽·▽·▽▽▽▽▼▼▽▽▽▽▽▽▽▽▼▼▽▽▽·▽·▽ ···Row 14
▽▽▽▼▼▽▽▽▽▽▽▽▽▽·▽·▽▽▽▽▽▼▼▽▽▽▽▽▽▼▼▽▽▽▽·▽·▽ ····Row 13
▽▽▽▼▼▽▽▽▽▽▽▽▽·▽·▽▽▽▽▽▼▼▽▽▽▽▽▽▼▼▽▽▽▽·▽·▽ ····Row 12
·▽·▽▽▼▼▽▽▽▽▽▽▽▽▽▽▽▽▽▽▼▼▽▽▽▽▽▽▽▼▼▽▽▽·▽· ····Row 11
·▽·▽▽▼▼▽▽▽▽▽▽▽▽▽▽▽▽▽▽▼▼▽▽▽▽▽▽▼▼▽▽▽▽·▽· ···Row 10
·▽·▽▽▼▼▽▽▽▽▽▽▽▽▽▽▽▽▽▽▼▼▽▽▽▽▽▽▼▼▽▽▽▽ ····Row 9
·▽·▽▽▽▽▽▽▽▽▽▽▽▽▽▽▽▽▽▽▼▼▽▽▽▽▽▽▼▼▽▽▽▽ ···Row 8
▽·▽·▽▽▽▽▽▽▽▽▽▽▽▽·▽·▽▽▽▽▽▽▼▼▽▽▽▽▽▽▼▼▽▽▽▽ ····Row 7
▽·▽·▽▽▽▽▽▽▽▽▽▽▽·▽·▽▽▽▽▽▼▼▽▽▽▽▽▽▽▼▼▽▽▽ ····Row 6
▽·▽·▽▽▽▽▽▽▽▽▽▽·▽·▽▽▽▽▽▽▼▼▽▽▽▽▽▽▽▼▼▽ Row 5
▽·▽·▽▽▽▽▽▽▼▽▽▽▽▽▽▽·▽·▽▽▽▽▼▼▽▽▽▽▽▽▽▽▼▼▽ ···Row 4
▽·▽·▽▽▽▽▽▽▽▼▽▽▽▽▽▽·▽·▽▽▽▽▼▼▽▽▽▽▽▽▽▽▼▼ ····Row 3
▽▽▽▽▽▽▽▽▽▽▽▽▽▽▽▽▽▽▽▽▽▽▽▽▽▽▽▽▽▽▽▽▽▽▽▽ ···Row 2
△△△△△△△△△△△△△△△△△△△△△△△△△△△△△△△△△△△△ Row 1
△△△△△△△△△△△△△△△△△△△△△△△△△△△△△△△△△△△△△ Reinforcement

——Join 35 pieces of 1st row in a ring.——

◁ ◁ ◁ ◁ ◁ ◁ ◁ ◁ ◁ ◁ ◁ ◁ ◁ ◁ ·················· ◁ ◁ ◁ ◁ ◁ ◁ ◁ ◁ ◁ ◁ ◁ ◁ ◁ ◁ ◁ ◁ ◁

RIM Join 33 pieces in a ring.

Turn over again and work until 14th round is done.

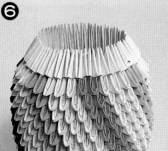
❺

On 15th round, reverse the direction of pieces.

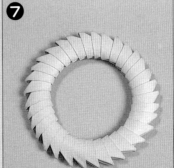
❻

Make rim by joining 33 pieces.

❼

Glue rim onto the vase to finish.

❽

1

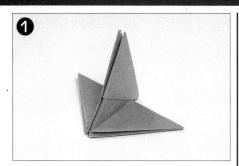

Place 2 pieces, pockets down, and the right angles away from you. Stack 1 piece on them, pockets down, in reverse direction.

2

Make 19 of this 3-piece unit. Join all the units in the same manner.

3

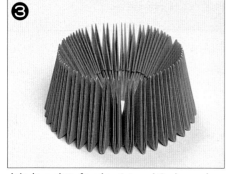

Join in a ring, forming 1st and 2nd rounds.

4

Turn over and reinforce the bottom by inserting 38 pieces all around.

5

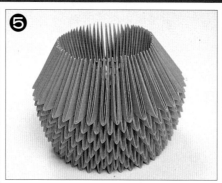

Showing when 9th round is done.

6

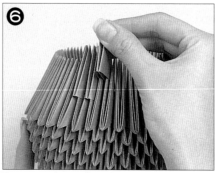

Reverse piece direction on 10th round.

7

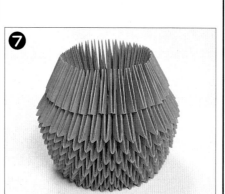

This is what it looks like after 10th round is done.

8

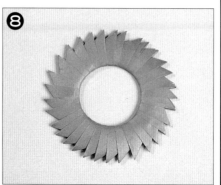

Make pedestal by joining 32 pieces in a ring.

9

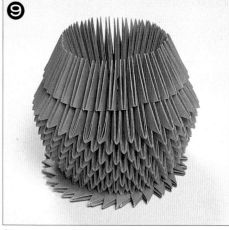

Glue pedestal to the bottom of vase.

10

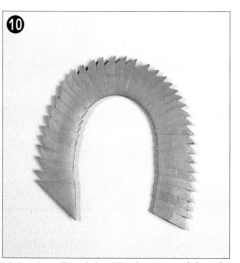

Make handle. Join 38 pieces and bend into U-letter shape.

11

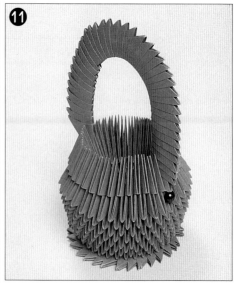

Insert handle in position, and glue on buttons to finish.